The Art *of* Mindful Gardening

Sowing The Seeds of Meditation

Ark Redwood

Leaping Hare Press

This paperback edition published in the UK in 2018 by
Leaping Hare Press
An imprint of The Quarto Group
The Old Brewery, 6 Blundell Street
London N7 9BH, United Kingdom
T (0)20 7700 6700 **F** (0)20 7700 8066
www.QuartoKnows.com

First published in hardback in 2011

British Library Cataloguing-in-Publication Data
A catalogue record for this book is available from the British Library

ISBN: 978-1-78240-583-2

This book was conceived, designed and produced by
Leaping Hare Press
58 West Street, Brighton BN1 2RA, United Kingdom

Creative Director PETER BRIDGEWATER
Publisher JASON HOOK
Commissioning Editor MONICA PERDONI
Art Director WAYNE BLADES
Senior Editor JAYNE ANSELL
Designer RICHARD CONSTABLE
Illustrators MELVYN EVANS, LYDIA CROOK

Printed in China

1 3 5 7 9 10 8 6 4 2

MIX
Paper from
responsible sources
FSC www.fsc.org FSC® C008047

CONTENTS

INTRODUCTION

◆

'Spring has hundreds of flowers; autumn, the clear moon.

Summer has cool winds; winter has snow.

If busyness doesn't take your mind,

That's your chance.'

FROM 'ESSENTIAL ZEN' BY KAZUAKI TANAHASHI & TENSHO DAVID SCHNEIDER
CASTLE BOOKS, 1994

◆

The art of being mindful is simple really. It lies in the practice of being in the present moment, and attempting to hold that attention to whatever you are doing, gently bringing the mind back to the present whenever it starts to wander (which it inevitably does!).

So simple, and yet it can take a lifetime, if not several lifetimes, to truly master. I, for one, certainly cannot claim to be anything but a novice in its application. Over the years I have been attempting to apply the practice of mindfulness to my own particular profession, which is that of a gardener; and it is the aim of this book to share some of the insights one may gain from applying them to this venerable craft of horticulture.

One thing this book is not is a gardening textbook. There are already countless volumes outlining the various and varied techniques necessary to be a successful gardener. The role of this particular book lies in suggesting ways to enhance your present moment awareness of whatever task you are engaged in, even the most seemingly mundane. I will also attempt to explain, in as simple terms as possible, the botanical reason that we do what we do in the garden.

Me Personally

I have been working professionally as a gardener since 1988. For the majority of that time I have had to focus my attention on learning as much as I can about plants, and how to grow and nurture them. It took me about ten years or so before I felt confident that I knew what I was talking about in regards to horticultural practice, and another ten before I realized that it was OK to admit that I didn't know everything! I used to liken being a gardener to being a doctor or a mechanic, in that people would always ask you questions that you would be expected to answer. Knowing that I still had gaps in my knowledge, I used to be very nervous that someone would 'catch me out'! These days I'm far more comfortable in not knowing the answers.

I think a lot of that comes from my growing practice of Buddhism, and particularly the huge influence on me of my spiritual teacher, Vietnamese Zen master Thich Nhat Hanh, who has, arguably, done more than anybody else in the Buddhist world to popularize the practice of mindfulness. His simple and clear approach to bringing awareness to the present moment is hugely compelling, and the insights he readily shares with his worldwide audience are very empowering; I am so grateful to him for teaching his wisdom to me, and countless other seekers around the globe.

An Oasis of Tranquillity

When it comes to having the opportunity to practise mindfulness in the garden, I do recognize that I am fortunate to work in a place that actively encourages such a mindset. Chalice Well Gardens, situated at the bottom of Glastonbury Tor, in the south-west of England, is a recognized World Peace Garden,

> 'In Buddhism, we go beyond the concepts of creation and destruction, of birth and death. We also go beyond the concepts of self and non-self. We have seen, for example, that a flower cannot "be" by itself alone. The flower cannot be. It can only inter-be. We must go back to what the Buddha said – "This is, because that is" – and train ourselves to look at things in the light of interdependence. We can see the entire universe in a flower. We can see not only the entire universe, but also all our ancestors and our children in every cell of our body.'
>
> FROM 'YOU ARE HERE' BY THICH NHAT HANH
> SHAMBHALA PRESS, 2009

dedicated to providing a refuge for all in a troubled world. By providing a sanctuary for people of all faiths, or none, it is an oasis of tranquillity, where visitors can come and feel nurtured by the healing vibrations so evident throughout the garden. There are many quiet spots for meditation, contemplation and spiritual reflection.

A Gentle Persistence

The exercises, practices and suggestions in this book are only pointers on the way, of course. Being fully in the present moment is not easy. In fact it takes a lot of focus and attention. Even Thich Nhat Hanh had to practise for decades to reach his current level of awareness. The word 'practice' is the key. We have to recognize that we are, after all, human beings, and the present society in which we live is not set up to encourage us to dwell fully in the present. The past and the future hold far greater sway in the public and cultural imagination. We should relish, and cherish, those times when we do manage to lose ourselves in the immediacy of present moment consciousness, however brief. The more we practise, the more fluent we'll become at holding our attention on the here and now. With all the myriad distractions bombarding us on a daily basis it's important not to be too hard on ourselves if we often fail to keep our concentration. If we beat ourselves up, and think we can't do it, then we won't. A gentle persistence will win through in the end.

'The breath is like a bridge that links our body and mind. If you come back to your breathing, your body and your mind begin to come back together again.'

FROM 'YOU ARE HERE' BY THICH NHAT HANH
SHAMBHALA PRESS, 2009

The Breath as an Anchor

In meditation practice, the breath is often used to hold the mind steady. This is because the breath is, along with our heartbeat, a constant rhythm throughout our lives. Most of the time we breathe quite unconsciously. 'Thank God,' you might say, 'imagine having to do it deliberately!' Quite! The point about the breath is that it can be utilized by our minds as an anchor upon which to hook our attention, and we can do this not just when we are in sitting meditation, but also when we are involved in an activity, such as walking, gardening or doing any exercise. Whenever attention wanders, we learn to bring it calmly back to the breath. The mind is a tricky customer; it doesn't want to be tamed. It would much rather be free to zigzag here, there and everywhere, and not be expected to stay concentrated on one thing at a time.

Instructing the Mind

The word 'discipline' is not exactly a popular word these days, as it smacks of being forced to do something you'd rather not, against your will. However, its root meaning is simply 'to instruct'. So we have to 'instruct' the mind to stay focused, and not shoot off in all directions. The mind eventually learns that one-pointedness actually feels quite good, and then it starts to yield to the discipline, thus becoming easier to tame. The key to this process is patience.

Gardening is a pastime that can give us a wealth of possibilities for mindfulness training, and I hope in this book to be able to suggest a few ways in which we can put them into practice for the benefit of our spiritual well-being, and help to serve us in other areas of our lives.

We have to 'instruct' the mind to stay focused, and not shoot off in all directions.

CHAPTER ONE

SPRING

*Something is stirring underfoot. Energy is
rising. The first green shoots appear. Expectation
is in the air. The first bumblebee is spotted, feeding
gratefully on early lungworts and hellebores.
Snowdrops ring out the changes. The birds serenade
our ears with their beautiful song. Time to grab our
coats and scarves, and venture forth into our little
bits of Eden. Being aware of our breath in the cold
air. Walking mindfully. Revelling in the promise
of a new year of abundance.*

THE SNOWDROP,
HERALD OF THE TURNING YEAR

◆

Every year I look forward to February — not just because I'm biased,
having been born in that month, but also because it is the season of
the snowdrop, a flower I love. When the snowdrops are in full bloom,
I feel the gardening year has truly begun.

THEIR LITTLE PEARL WHITE BELLS, flecked with green,
seem to herald in the promise of the new, ringing out
that change is in the air, and the gardener had better prepare
for a steadily increasing presence in the garden. The snowdrop is like a floral mindfulness bell, reminding us that the
earth is beginning to breathe out again after the slumbers of
winter, calling us to follow our own breath mindfully as we
eagerly anticipate the horticultural labours to come.

February – The First Month of Spring?

February always used to be considered a month associated
with wintertime, and I suppose to a lot of people it still is.
However, with the climate chaos associated with the phenomenon of global warming, it feels more and more like the first
month of spring.

February actually gets its name from the Latin *februa*,
meaning 'to purify', and if we approach this time of year in
that spirit it gives us an opportunity to look at ways we may

need to purify our own lives and practices. In the garden we can clear out our sheds, clean tools, sort through old flower-pots, dispose of old seed packets, give cold frames and greenhouses a thorough clean, or gather up stuff from our home that we wish to let go, and then light up a small bonfire to burn it all away. After such activity we often feel refreshed and cleansed as we let go of the legacy of the past, turning our sights to the future still to come.

As February moves into March, the first glimmerings of green gradually gather pace and there is a quickening of energies apparent everywhere. This is the time to venture out into the garden to prepare for the onrush of activity that is just around the corner.

SHAPING UP

One job that is calling out to be done at this time of year is forma-tive pruning and shaping of shrubs. This is a subject that a lot of people feel unconfident about, and can result in the plant not getting as thorough a prune as it requires.

OFTEN, PERHAPS WHEN A SHRUB HAS BEEN NEGLECTED over the years, people feel it is 'cruel' to give it the necessary hard prune that it so obviously needs. I think we have to accept that gardening is, as an activity, clearly a human interference into the lives and rhythms of living beings. Saying that, I feel that, although this is strictly true, we humans have to ensure that when we do 'interfere', we do so with as much care and consciousness as we can muster. After all, in truth, if all things are interdependently connected, as the wise ones throughout history proclaim, then we cannot consider ourselves as separate from the rest of creation. There is no separation between the garden and the gardener.

If we practise our gardening with mindfulness and love, we can surely only enhance the quality of life of the plants and creatures with whom we share this planet. So if, as we reach for our secateurs, shears and loppers, we have an understanding of what it is we are actually going to do when we cut off branches and twigs, then the greater our gardening insight will be, and the more the individual shrub will benefit.

Mindful Pruning

When a plant is focused on growth in its early stages, energy is concentrated primarily in the leader shoots, i.e. the terminal buds of the outer and upper stems. The hormones that trigger growth are usually suppressed in the lower buds. This is to ensure the plant against being grazed or damaged. The plant aims to put maximum effort into reaching its full potential. In the event of the terminal buds being cut off, the hormones are released lower down, and the plant continues growing from its side shoots, creating a more bushy shape. This is exactly what happens when we prune or shape a shrub. Therefore, armed with this knowledge, we can engage in mindful pruning, aware of what we are doing, and have some understanding of what is happening to the plant while we do so.

The Five Ds

If pruning, as an activity, is something you feel unconfident pursuing, then perhaps I can suggest a very easy formula which you can apply to almost all plants, especially trees and shrubs. If you follow it, then you will have no problem convincing other people (including yourself) that you know what you are doing! This is known as the five Ds. They are: Dead & Dying, Diseased & Deformed (i.e. Damaged), and Direction.

So, if faced with an old, neglected apple tree (for instance), stand back and really look at it; regard its needs, and how you might restore its dignity. Begin to apply the five Ds. Start by searching for the dead, and obviously dying, branches, and saw them off; next do the same to those that are looking riven with disease, or are damaged in any way. This will have served to open up the crown of the tree a little, which will give you a chance to spot those branches that are pointing inwards or crossing other, more well-placed, limbs (i.e. pointing outwards). These represent the fifth D of Direction, so lop them off.

What you will end up with is a much more open canopy, thereby ensuring better circulation of air and light, something that is vital for all healthy plants. Also, you may be able to sense a lightening in the energy of the tree, which you would be quite entitled to translate as a big 'thank you' for taking the time to tend to its needs. A horticultural demonstration of compassion in action!

EXERCISE 1

PRUNING MEDITATION

- Stand in front of the shrub to be pruned…
- Centre yourself by focusing on your breath…
- Be aware of your body, feel the ground beneath your feet…
- Sense any air movements on your face and skin. Be where you are…
- Look closely at the shrub. Feel its presence before you…
- Send it love…
- With your imagination, picture the energy flow within the structure of the plant…
- Mindfully reach for your secateurs, and feel their weight in your hand…
- Still visualizing the flow of energy, decide on the height you want to cut to and snip off above a bud…
- Visualize the energy flowing now out of the side buds…
- Continue until you feel satisfied the job has been done…
- Try to maintain a constant awareness of your breath throughout this meditation.

SEEDS OF CONSCIOUSNESS

◆

'As a gardener, we have to trust the land, knowing
that all seeds of love and understanding, seeds of
enlightenment and happiness, are already there.'

FROM 'CULTIVATING THE MIND OF LOVE' BY THICH NHAT HANH
PARALLAX PRESS, 1996

◆

*As a horticulturist, one of the great joys of the job is propagation,
particularly sowing seeds. I never tire of it, however many years I've
been doing so. Every springtime I am thrilled when I see the tiny seed
leaves first appearing on the surface of the seed tray.*

THERE IS SOMETHING MAGICAL ABOUT GERMINATION,
and I cannot see how anyone can fail to be delighted to
welcome the manifestation of new life. I experience a tide of
tenderness washing over me whenever I see those little green
specks on the surface of the compost, and I make a silent vow
to guide the infant seedlings to maturity, as if they were my
own children. No wonder it's called a 'nursery'!

Seeds really are amazing. They carry within their minuscule
bodies all that the future plant requires to fuel it for growth,
except water. The genetic blueprint can be likened to an
ancestral stream flowing through the plant, connecting it with
all of its kin, both in the past and on to future generations. The
seed does not just come into being from nowhere; it is more

> 'The seeds of negativity are always there, but
> very positive seeds also exist, such as the seeds of
> compassion, tolerance, and love. These seeds are all
> there in the soil. But without rain they cannot manifest.
> Our practice is to recognize and water the positive seeds.
> If you recognize the seed of compassion in yourself, you
> should make sure it is watered several times a day.'
>
> FROM 'YOU ARE HERE' BY THICH NHAT HANH
> SHAMBHALA PRESS, 2009

a continuation from its parents, just like us. The right conditions have now come together for the seed to manifest, and here it is in all its glory!

Storehouses of Well-being

When you think about it, it's remarkable how inextricably linked seeds are with human history – after all, the staple diets of almost all cultures are seeds or derived from seeds, e.g. rice, wheat, sorghum, rye, quinoa, barley, corn, oats, etc. The concentrated energy and wholesome goodness found in grains has ensured that they have had a huge role to play in our development as a species. For this reason alone we should never cease to be thankful for these splendid little storehouses of health and well-being.

So when you sow a seed, it is good practice to be really aware of just what it is that you are doing. The gardener is adding the final ingredients before green life can manifest, i.e. water, plus a medium to grow it in, be that compost or garden soil. Try to be conscious of the fact that, in a way, the gardener is acting as a midwife to new life being brought into the world. By adding the truly magical substance of water, you are providing the last link in an alchemical chain of becoming. Finally, the process of manifestation is triggered, a fresh green being arises out of the pregnant earth, and a new note is sounded in the symphony of life.

ENLIGHTENMENT DAY BY DAY

Plants are not just unintelligent, static, unfeeling organisms. They possess unique abilities to respond to their environment in often the most delicate of ways. Their sensitivity to subtle differences in light levels and day length is remarkable, and it is this ability that triggers their most vital responses to the promptings of life.

I F I WERE ASKED WHAT I THOUGHT was the most magical and mysterious phenomenon on Earth, I would not hesitate to say 'photosynthesis'. This seemingly miraculous transformation of sunlight into carbohydrates to fuel growth still serves to baffle biologists. Nobody has ever come near to fully explaining just how plants actually do it. Without photosynthesis, life would probably have stayed at the purely microbial, and we would not be here to bear witness to the fantastic variety of plant and animal species.

The link between light and life is plain to all when we annually witness the connection of increasing day length and the arising of plants from the deep slumber of winter. By early spring, the first glimmerings of green gather momentum as roots rise up out of the dark womb of the Earth, transmuting themselves into shoots. Soon, leaves unfurl their varied shapes and begin to wave to the Sun like so many solar-panelled flags, twisting and turning as they efficiently convert the rays of light into sugars to fuel further growth.

A Leaf Contemplation

Sometime in the midst of all this, on a bright and sunny day (perhaps in mid-March when the process is gathering pace), it's a good idea to stand and pause a while in the garden in order to revel in this energetic dance of cellular enlightenment.

Find a tree, shrub, newly arising perennial or spring bulb and regard it closely, attempting to visualize the process of photosynthesis, in whichever way makes sense to you, and marvel at it. Hold a leaf, freshly green, up to the light and observe its network of veins. Feel the vibrant delight of the plant as it gratefully soaks up the solar energy suffusing it from every direction. Recognize that any apparent separation between it and the Sun is actually an illusion. All is One. There is just the dance, the cosmic dance, playing out before our eyes. Sometimes, if we can put aside our preconceptions, it is possible to lose ourselves in this realization and a sort of rapture envelops us. Our awareness expands to include all that is. We experience a joyful, yet familiar, recognition that there is only the thinnest of veils between our everyday consciousness and this universal awareness. Our Buddha nature laid bare. And all this from a simple meditation on a leaf!

'Plants can remember stimuli, and tell one form of stimulus from another. They can communicate, and they cooperate to survive. If plants required more intelligence, they would have developed it. As it is, their senses and the limits of their sentience are exactly what they require. Some of the senses in the plant world are already more highly developed than ours (the sense of touch, for example). No longer should science regard a green plant as a simple organism which endures what it must, and adjusts like a chemical system. We owe plants respect, for on green plants we all rely for survival. They are not our subjects; plants are our cousins.'

FROM 'THE SECRET LANGUAGE OF LIFE: HOW ANIMALS
AND PLANTS FEEL AND COMMUNICATE' BY BRIAN J. FORD
FROMM INTERNATIONAL, 2000

MONTHLY MUSINGS

◆

I pondered earlier upon the derivation of the word 'February', and attempted to suggest ways we may connect with its root meaning of 'purity' and 'purification' in order to reflect its energy in our own lives, while being held within its cold embrace.

NOW I FEEL I SHOULD DO LIKEWISE with the next three months of the year. Firstly, I must say that I do find that being conscious of the correspondence between the time of year and one's inner journey is quite compelling, and I am also grateful that our names for the first six months lend themselves so readily to this contemplation. It is a bit less applicable to the final half of the year as the names were Latinized by the Romans. However, I'm sure that the same insights can be applied from July to December, given that all the months reflect their special qualities within the natural cycle as the Earth makes her journey around the Sun. (I am very conscious that these musings only really make sense with regards to the northern hemisphere. I will therefore leave it to our Antipodean cousins to offer their own interpretation!)

March Winds

The month of March (Mars), as most people quite rightly assume, was dedicated in honour of the eponymous Roman god of war. However, before he acquired his more martial connotations, Mars was originally an agricultural deity associated with the power of the wind, especially in its ability to blow away the old, clearing the ground for the new. There is still an echo of this in our practice of 'spring cleaning'. Certainly outside in the garden we experience the effects of these 'March winds' as they sweep away the old debris from the previous year, clearing spaces in our beds and borders, and encouraging us to grab a trowel and get weeding. So as these 'winds of change' blow across the garden we can start planning how to fill these gaps, and begin the process of designing a planting plan, at least in our mind's eye, in order to maximize the space for as long a growing season as we can, whether that be in the ornamental garden or the allotment.

March is a fickle month; often we experience days of blue skies and bright sun warming our backs, encouraging us to think that summer is here; then as soon as we start assuming it's safe to break out the T-shirts it's back to cold, grey skies with lashings of freezing rain soaking us to the skin. Perhaps the keyword for March is 'patience', or maybe even 'impatience'. However, warmer days are just around the corner, and that gives us hope that the year has at last sprung into spring.

April Showers

April is also fickle, but at least we know that the days are definitely getting longer, as we've now got lighter evenings to tend our gardens, and there is far less of a chill in the air.

It derives its name from the Latin word *aperio*, meaning 'to open'. I see it as referring to the buds of trees and shrubs gradually opening out to unfurl their leaves, freshly green with the promise of new life. There is an eagerness in the air, and everywhere hope and optimism are bursting out all over the natural world and yet tuning into the quality of stillness.

In the garden there is a sense that warmer days are coming, and even when it rains we will fondly welcome these 'April showers' because we recognize their importance at this time of the year in providing plenty of moisture for our new seedlings and young plants. There is a lot of activity all around, and I have often believed that April is the busiest month for gardeners, especially for those with greenhouses or polytunnels.

However, within all this constant flurry of 'busyness' it is also a good idea to stop and take stock of where we are within the cycle of the year. The contrast between the burgeoning buds, the full-on nature of all the jobs to do, and the quality of stillness is a good practice.

EXERCISE 2

FEELING FRESH

• Find a place where this energy of opening is very active and obvious, perhaps a local woodland or your own garden, and either stand or sit, keeping your eyes open.

• Bring your focus to your breath. While breathing in, be aware of breathing in; while breathing out, be aware of breathing out.

• Do this until you feel calm and relaxed.

• Focus now on your body posture, keeping your back straight.

• Feel the ground beneath you, and the sky above you.

• Sense the movement of air around you, on your hands, head and face, and on your clothes.

• Look around at all the leaves of the trees and shrubs opening out to begin their annual dance with the elements of life and being.

• Observe the perennial plants emerging out of the ground as they awaken from their slumbers underground.

• Feel the freshness all around. How does your body respond to this feeling?

• Tune in to your own hopes and aspirations for the year. Are you ready to open out the buds of new possibilities in your own life?

• Try not to get too analytical and thought-centred. Keep open to your instinctual and your intuitive responses to this question.

• All the while, maintain awareness of your breath.

• When you feel you wish to break this spell, come back into your body and, bringing your palms together, gently bow to your surroundings.

The Merry Month of May

If there were a candidate for the most popular month, then May would certainly have a good case to answer. There's not much you can say against this glorious time of year. Everything is just so full of life, and the garden often looks at its most vibrant. The name of the month certainly suggests this, as it ultimately derives from the Sanskrit word mag, meaning 'to grow', from where we get words like 'magnify' and 'magnificent'. This is also from where the Roman goddess of spring, Maia, gets her name.

This energy of rampant growth can sometimes feel overwhelming; no wonder so many gardeners seek refuge in their sheds! However, this is not really a time for hiding away. There's far too much to do. I often find myself zigzagging around the garden doing a bit of this, then a bit of that. Sometimes I almost bump into myself!

Beltane Revels

In pagan Europe, the beginning of the month of May (otherwise known as Beltane) was a time of great celebration and many fertility rites were enacted, including a temporary loosening of the social strictures on overt sexuality, whereby young couples would often disappear off to the nearest hayrick in order to indulge in a ritual of the more licentious kind!

Now, of course, I am not in any way suggesting that the mindful gardener, in order to be authentic, should do likewise, but I am hinting that there is a lot of sexual imagery in nature at this time of the year, which may interest those of a particularly fertile imagination.

After all, what are flowers if not the sexual organs of plants wafting their pheromones in the air, eager to flirt with any insect that happens to be flying by. No wonder the Victorians viewed botanical illustration as somewhat risqué.

THE MAGIC OF COMPOST, OR THE TAO OF POO

◆

'The dance of impermanence extends beyond the physical
world to the mind and states of consciousness. Consciousness
itself is impermanent. To reach the state where there is
no becoming, one must accept that everything, absolutely
everything, is always becoming. This experience leads to one of
the central teachings in Buddhism: the teaching of emptiness...
When the depth of our helplessness is realized, we find peace.'

BY ELIZABETH ROBERTS, FROM 'DHARMA GAIA: A HARVEST OF ESSAYS
IN BUDDHISM AND ECOLOGY', EDITED BY ALLAN HUNT BADINER
PARALLAX PRESS, 1990

◆

Compost is an alchemical potion of form and substance, fertility and vibrant potential. It is a curiously magical mixture of both composition and decomposition; filled with life, and yet formed from death. A potent brew indeed!

A GOOD JOB TO DO ON A CHILLY MORNING in spring is to turn the compost heap, i.e. move it from one bay, or pile, to an adjoining one. It will soon get the blood pumping around your body and warm up those weary muscles. Please don't do so reluctantly, grumbling that you can't see the point as it will all rot down anyway without you having to raise a pitchfork in assistance. This is magic work. A well-made compost heap is truly alchemy in action. Although you can just pile up organic matter in a heap on the ground, which will eventually decompose, it is worthwhile tuning in to what makes a good compost, as opposed to an indifferent one.

What is Compost?

First, it might be a good idea to consider what compost actually is. First of all, no two composts are the same, although they all consist of various forms of organic material pressed together; over time, this forms a rich, dark brown substance, full of nutrients, which is added to the soil to enhance the growth of our garden plants. Sounds simple, but it is definitely worth giving some consideration to just what goes into the heap. Some things are best left out of the mixture, e.g. invasive weed roots (bindweed, ground elder, couch grass, nettles, etc.); garden soil (this can dilute the composting process if added in quantity); and food scraps such as leftover meat and oils, which could attract rats. Leftover steamed or boiled vegetables are fine, however.

Play it Safe

What you are aiming for is a good consistency, so be sure to mix up any grass cuttings with more fibrous material such as stems, larger weeds, shredded newspaper or straw. Do try to avoid putting weed seeds on the compost, because although it is often quoted that the seeds are 'cooked' by the composting process, this is only true if you can guarantee a high temperature; most domestic heaps rarely achieve this. So it is best if you play safe and adopt a purist approach. Otherwise you could end up simply re-infecting your garden with the very weeds you have just dug up.

A Source of Delight

Personally, I find the whole process of composting a never-ending source of delight and fascination. Although it can take a relatively long time to reach the desired result, the act of gradually adding differing organic materials to the mix over a period of several months, and watching it slowly rot down, is something I relish (or maybe I'm just mad!). I very often add my old clothes (as long as they are one hundred per cent natural fibre, such as wool, cotton or hemp). To think that these will one day turn into flowers or vegetables is a wonderful and thought-provoking thing to consider.

What a compost heap basically does is break down organic matter into its core constituents, be that carbon, nitrogen, hydrogen, potassium, etc. Later, these same elements are redistributed into our beds and borders, and over time they are taken up by the root hairs of plants to re-combine into new forms. In nature, this process happens whenever top growth dies back in the winter and falls to the ground. The same organisms are attracted to the site, and the composting sequence kicks in. All we as gardeners do is concentrate this deceased top growth into a deliberate heap and encourage these organisms to work for our benefit.

> 'Only a true gardener knows the satisfaction
> which comes from creating a delicious mound of
> top quality compost, which crumbles freely in
> the hand and looks like centuries old peat, rich,
> dark, sweet-smelling, moist and friable. It's a
> primordial pleasure which rekindles awareness
> of our utter dependence on the natural cycle of
> regeneration and re-use. Every time we handle a
> lump of compost we are reminded that the earth
> is not dead, but pulsating with life.'
>
> FROM 'THE THERAPEUTIC GARDEN' BY DONALD NORFOLK
> BANTAM PRESS, 2000

Gardeners' Gold

The key players in all this are billions of bacteria which, along with a myriad of other tiny organisms, spend their days gloriously consuming decaying matter and transforming it into what is quite rightly often referred to as 'gardeners' gold'. Compost is far from being a dead substance. If you were to peer at it through a powerful microscope you would observe a constantly active, vibrant world. If you haven't got access to one of those, just try a good magnifying glass, and you will be able to watch numerous invertebrates scuttling about on the surface, getting on with the business of frantically exploring their world, looking out for juicy titbits while attempting to avoid the attentions of predators who just might be lurking around every nook and cranny.

Hot Stuff

Turning compost is not only good exercise on a chilly morning, it is also essential if the goal is eventually to have good consistency of decomposition throughout the heap.

The initial pile of organic matter will quickly heat up as the bacteria 'leap' into action. (To experience this, stick a bamboo cane deep into the centre of the pile when you first create the heap, and when you've got a good amount withdraw it, and feel the temperature of the cane. Be warned, it can get very hot! This is actually a good practice to test how your friendly bacteria are doing.) After a period of time it will naturally begin to cool down, as bacterial action slows down. As it does so, other organisms, such as worms, slugs, woodlice and countless invertebrates, take up the challenge and add their contribution to breaking down the heap, and it noticeably shrinks in size as gravity pulls tight the air pockets.

Turn, Turn, Turn...

Like a bowl of soup the heap is hotter in the middle, and this is where decomposition is most effective; therefore, in order to encourage the bacteria to get to work again on the cooler sides, the compost is subsequently 'turned'. So, with this in mind, it is always a good idea to have an empty bay next to your 'working' one.

As you fork it over from one bay to the next, try to deposit the middle to the sides, and the sides to the middle (although please don't become too obsessed with this). This action will help to even out the rotting process. Most compost heaps require about three or four turnings, so there is plenty of scope for further exercise!

I often liken turning a compost heap to stirring a cauldron, as really that is exactly what you are doing. You are alchemically transmuting forms of things into other forms, and in the process virtually proving that nothing really dies, it just continues on living in other ways and shapes. The compost you're creating will be used in the life cycle of another being. Today's flowers are tomorrow's cabbages.

Some Things Just Don't Mix

One other thing to note is that it is generally not a good idea
to mix together green organic materials and tree leaves. They
require different conditions for effective decomposition.
Green leaves are generally soft-bodied and require bacterial
action in order to be broken down, plus a warm and moist
environment, while tree leaves need fungal action, and cool

'If you look deeply at a flower, at its freshness
and its beauty, you will also see that there is compost
in it, made of garbage. The gardener has the skill to
transform this garbage into compost, and with this
compost, he made a flower grow.

Flowers and garbage are both organic in nature.
So looking deeply into the presence of the compost
and the garbage, the flower is also going to turn into
garbage; but don't be afraid! You are a gardener,
and you have in your hands the power to transform
garbage into flowers, into fruit, into vegetables. You
don't throw anything away, because you are not afraid
of garbage. Your hands are capable of transforming
it into flowers, lettuce or cucumbers.'

FROM 'YOU ARE HERE' BY THICH NHAT HANH
SHAMBHALA PRESS, 2009

and moist conditions. If tree leaves were as soft as the leaves of other green plants they would probably soon be shredded by the storms that often buffet the canopies of trees, and the tree would have to expend a lot of energy producing replacement leaves. To avoid this, the tree produces a substance called lignin, and concentrates it in the veins of the tree leaves, therefore providing a tough skeleton for protection against high winds. Lignin is very hard, and bacteria would struggle to break it down, whereas fungi have no such problem.

Separate Rooms

Make sure your tree leaves and other green materials go into different containers (a wire mesh leaf cage is ideal for tree leaves). Remember that as green material usually comes from living or recently living organisms, it contains a fair amount of nutrients and the compost from this is great for feeding plants, whereas tree leaves have had all the nutrients taken from them prior to falling to the ground, and therefore after decomposition the resulting leaf mould is better used for soil conditioning, rather than for fertilizing plants.

I hope that now I've tried to explain a little more about the magical qualities of compost there will be no hesitation in grabbing a garden fork, rushing outside on a cold spring day and relishing the opportunity to expend a bit of physical energy (mindfully, of course), in the pursuit of the holy grail of the 'gardener's gold'.

THE DEVIC REALM

◆

The mindful gardener would do well to recognize that there are formative energies within nature that are not readily apparent to our 'ordinary' five senses; that these forces play a pivotal role in the creation of all that we see in the natural world around us, and it would be unwise simply to dismiss them as mere fantasy.

THE PRINCIPAL PURPOSE OF THIS BOOK is to encourage gardeners to be fully conscious of what they are doing, and to accomplish their gardening tasks as mindfully as possible. This takes into account not just being aware of your breath and posture, but also the botanical reasons behind our horticultural endeavours. This way, a more rounded and informed mindfulness can be achieved.

The emphasis so far has been primarily focused on the physical world, the world familiar to our senses and everyday consciousness. However, I believe there is another world, operating in and around the physical dimension, which I would like to touch on now. This is the world of the devas and nature spirits, which inform so much of what we see and feel all around us. I am, of course, aware that belief in the existence of these beings is controversial, and I can understand why some readers may start to glaze over right now, but I would like to ask you to hang on in there while I expand upon this theme, and maybe I can shed some light on this subject.

Encounters with Elementals

Ever since the well-documented role they were believed to
have played in the foundation of the famous Findhorn
community, in the north-east of Scotland, in the 1960s, a lot
has been written about devas and nature spirits, and the world
of the elementals, and the crucial part they play in the growth
and maintenance of the various life forms of the planet. Like
many people, I have been fascinated by the stories told of
encounters with these beings, and over the years I have more
and more accepted the reality of their existence, and have
attempted to use various ways to try to communicate with
them. I do not profess to be able actually to see these beings
(not possessing clairvoyant vision), but I would perhaps admit
to being clairsentient, in that I can feel their energetic presence,

'There are many universal truths of nature,
which may be expressed as doorways connecting one
realm to another. In seeking them we encounter one
world that is visible and another buried beneath it,
which may be seen only if we look very closely. True
consciousness is the ability to see all worlds of nature,
for there is order to every aspect of the universe.'

FROM 'ROOTED IN THE SPIRIT: EXPLORING
INSPIRATIONAL GARDENS' BY MAUREEN GILMER
TAYLOR PUBLISHING COMPANY, 1997

especially in highly charged places, such as the Chalice Well Gardens where I work. This is often characterized by a sense of what I call 'hushness', which is apparent in places of power, where magic is afoot. Of course, I am not alone in this as many people possess this sense of awareness, and interpret their impressions in their own way. So this is just my current understanding of the way these creative powers contribute to the unfoldment of being.

Architects and Builders

I see the devas, nature spirits and elementals as the personification of the creative forces of nature. The elementals govern the energies of the four elements of earth, air, fire and water which make up the physical world all around us, personalized in British folklore as gnomes, sylphs, salamanders and undines respectively, although other cultures have their own equivalents. The devas are a bit like architects who hold the etheric blueprint of a particular species; they 'inform' the perfect plant, and will maintain this attention throughout its lifetime. The nature spirits, the builders, as it were, then utilize this 'information' provided by the devas, to bring the plant from the etheric into the physical realm.

A Fruitful Relationship

For instance, if you sow the seed of, say, a carrot, the creative forces come into play, and a devic blueprint of a perfect carrot is superimposed in and around the seed. The forces of manifestation (i.e. the nature spirits) then attempt to bring that idea of the perfect carrot from the etheric into the physical. This is why it is beholden on the wise gardener to provide the optimum conditions possible for the seed to grow into the 'perfect' plant. The nature spirits can only do this well if they are provided with the right environment for the individual species. It would be difficult for them to have to nurture a moisture-loving plant if the soil is continually bone dry. The physical form of the plant would inevitably suffer, and the potential for pests and diseases would be greatly increased. A plant provided with optimum conditions for its survival will always thrive, and emit a 'happier' vibration, therefore helping it to maintain health and vigour. So the key to a partnership between the gardener and the devic realm is for the former always to be sensitive to the requirements of the latter. That way, a fruitful relationship can be guaranteed.

It is beholden on the wise gardener to provide the optimum conditions possible for the seed to grow into the 'perfect' plant.

The Perfect Plant

Only once have I ever come across what I would claim to be a 'perfect' plant, and this was one that ordinarily a gardener would not hesitate to pluck out as a 'useless' weed. Before I took up my current post at Chalice Well I was a jobbing gardener, employed by a variety of customers around my local area. One garden I looked after was a two-acre plot, consisting of different areas and habitats, the two principal sections being divided by a small wooded area, which was usually left to its own devices.

One late spring day as I was walking through a clearing in this copse my attention was drawn to a plant which normally I would have had no hesitation in weeding, in order to prevent it eventually blowing its seeds everywhere. It was a common 'weed' called the prickly sowthistle (Sonchus asper). There was something about it that was striking, and that was that it was perfect in every way, with not a blemish. It emitted a real presence the like of which I have never seen in a plant before, or since. Needless to say I didn't weed it out. Instead I just watched it grow through the summer, and every time I passed it I would give it a respectful bow, and often would verbally praise it. Never did it lose its vibrancy, and to this day I have never come across a plant with such a high frequency of vibration. And all this in an ordinary common 'weed'!

THE LIVING SOIL

◆

'Having empathy for others, one sees

that all beings love life, and fear death.

Knowing this, one does not attack or cause attack.

To harm living beings who, like us, seek

contentment, is to bring harm to ourselves.

To avoid bringing harm to living beings who, like us,

seek contentment, is to bring happiness to ourselves.'

FROM 'A DHAMMAPADA FOR CONTEMPLATION',
TRANSLATED BY AJAHN MUNEDHO
ARUNA PUBLICATIONS, 2006

◆

It is one of the arts of the mindful gardener to try to provide the perfect place for plants to flourish. One of the key ingredients to a healthy garden is a well-structured soil and it is wise to recognize just how crucial this is to a holistic approach to horticulture.

A LOT OF GARDEN PLANTS PREFER a moisture-retentive, yet free-draining, fairly fertile medium in which to grow, although other species have different requirements. It would be a case of horticultural cruelty to insist that a bog plant should grow on sand, for example, or a sunflower should put up with a situation of deep shade.

Before any area is planted up, it is wise to look at the soil quality and structure, to consider whether the prospective plants would thrive, or diminish, if placed there, and to take any remedial action necessary.

To Dig or Not to Dig? – That is the Question

There is a generation of gardeners (those who grew up during the 1940s and 50s), influenced by the famous 'Dig for Victory' campaigns of the Second World War, who would not think twice about grabbing their trusty spades, happily venturing outside, thoroughly digging over the ground and cheerfully putting their backs into it (and, it must be said, often putting their backs out!).

Now, this may have served as good exercise on a cold and frosty day, but it is not necessarily good horticultural practice. For soil is not just an inert collection of minerals, but a vibrant community of organisms all living at different layers, and for the most part doing so harmoniously (which does not preclude the everyday battles between pest and predator). All this is ongoing provided the soil is left undisturbed.

Digging with a spade (i.e. inverting the soil) is not the way to go if you want to encourage a living soil.

When to Use a Spade

Obviously this does not mean that spades are to be considered defunct as a useful tool, and banished for ever from the tool shed. There will be instances when it is justifiable to dig over the ground in order to add leaf mould or compost, such as in instances of poor quality, overly stony patches, or in areas of thick, impenetrable clay. Also a spade is, of course, the correct tool for planting trees and shrubs, as it is obvious that a hole will be required.

When Not to Use a Spade

Most creatures that live in the soil do so at particular depths that suit them best, and so if we disturb their world we can end up killing them (or at least causing them a lot of confusion!). The majority of earthworms, for instance, if left to their own devices, seldom venture above the 10-centimetre (3-inch) level. It is only when we turn over the soil that we see them, and also, it must be said, expose them to the attentions of any passing garden bird.

A lot of these creatures can, however, cope with small scale disturbances to their environment, so trowels and hand forks for weeding purposes are fine, and in cases where a spade would have been used in the past, try to substitute a garden fork, as this tends to pose less of a problem to the citizens of the soil, bearing in mind that inversion should be kept to a minimum. The kindest way to incorporate organic matter is to layer the surface with a mulch and let nature's best diggers, the earthworms, do the job for you. It may take longer to achieve your goal, but this is not only better for your back muscles, it is also better for maintaining and enhancing biodiversity, something for which every gardener should strive.

THE QUICKENING

◆

'Plants are bursting with movement. They are rich
in sensation, and respond to the stimulation of the
surrounding world every moment of their active lives.
They can send messages to each other about overcrowding
or a threatened attack by a new pest. Within each plant
there is ceaseless activity as purposive as that in an animal.
Many of them share hormones that are remarkably similar
to our own. Their senses are sophisticated: some can detect
the lightest touch (better than the sensitivity of the human
fingertips), and they all have a sense of vision.'

FROM 'THE SECRET LANGUAGE OF LIFE: HOW ANIMALS
AND PLANTS FEEL AND COMMUNICATE' BY BRIAN J. FORD
FROMM INTERNATIONAL, 2000

◆

*Spring is a time of hope and aspiration. As the days steadily grow
longer, life just seems to speed up, and we gardeners reach our busiest
time of the year. The demands of our little patch of earth call out to
us daily, and it can sometimes be hard to keep up with it all.*

THE NORTHERN HEMISPHERE rapidly cloaks herself with
her green mantle, and her outbreath is almost audible.
The bell shapes of spring bulbs ring loud the clarion call of
nature's promised bounty. As the sun's rays increase in
strength, the tentative rise of energy from roots to shoots,

first heralded in early February, gathers pace as March gives way to April, and May beckons brightly. This is a good time to try to find opportunities to stop every now and then to pause and marvel amid the splendour of it all.

A Time to Stand and Stare

Take time out to go and stare at the buds breaking fresh and newly green from twigs of hawthorn; try to keep up with a bumblebee as it flits from one early flower to another, and watch closely how it fills its swollen pollen sacs; observe with wonder the sight of a seemingly freshly shrivelled-up petal of a poppy, squashed into its flower bud, gradually and miraculously unfurling itself; or focus your attention over an extended period of time on the gradually rising crescendo of birdsong as our avian cousins prepare for nesting.

As you follow the natural cycle closely, with all of your senses more and more keenly attuned, you may observe in yourself a rising tide of joy, echoing the natural world, and the illusory boundary between your supposedly independent, separate self and the environment around you will begin to diminish daily. You can then, hopefully, engage with your work in the garden more connected to, and at one with, the seasonal cycles of nature.

Domestic Help

Be aware also that, for most of the animals – especially the invertebrates – within 'your' garden, this is their home. You have a responsibility to care for their world. So during the spring months they will be actively seeking out new nesting sites to rear their next generation. You can help them by providing potential habitats – nest boxes for birds, bug boxes for ladybirds and lacewings, upturned clay flowerpots for bumblebees, and areas of long grass for ground beetles. If you can create as much biodiversity as possible within the garden, then you should keep damage from so-called pests to a minimum, by encouraging the presence of predators.

The other vital truth to recognize is that there is no separation between the garden and the gardener. It is not the case that you are, as an individual, divided from your surroundings. The world 'out there' does not begin at the end of your skin. This is a holistic universe, and all is truly One.

There is no separation between the garden and the gardener.

CHAPTER TWO

SUMMER

There is burgeoning growth all around.
Joy fills the air as all beings celebrate Life.
Sap has well and truly risen, and the garden appears
to be bursting with kaleidoscopic colour. Solstice marks
the high point of the year when all around seems full
of exuberance and gratitude. The warming rays of the
sun on our backs fill us with blissful contentment.
Amid all the frantic activity we find time to pause,
and give thanks. Abundance beckons.

WALKING THE GARDEN PATH

◆

One activity we are nearly always engaged in, wherever we are working, is the simple act of walking. Most of us don't give it a second thought, and regard it only as an unremarkable method to get from A to B. However, it can be a way to connect with the deepest parts of ourselves and in this busy season we need that balance.

THE END OF SPRING and the early part of summer is a time of year when being a gardener can often seem overwhelming. There is just so much to do – weeding and hoeing, watering, propagating, moving plants from the potting shed to the greenhouse, and then on to the cold frame, before finally planting them out in their predetermined place in the garden or allotment. It can be so busy that we fail to take time out, losing ourselves in the flurry of things to do, and we fail to maintain contact with the present moment.

The key lies in attention. Often when we walk we aren't even aware of our legs moving, so intent are we on our destination. Walking meditation can bring us back to the present moment by combining concentrative action with the one-pointedness of meditation. A gardener has ample opportunity to practise it, as distance doesn't really matter with this technique. Whether you are walking up the garden path, stepping from greenhouse to cold frame, or taking three steps from one bed to the next, you can avail yourself of this exercise.

'In both a literal and a figurative way, a garden can help us come to our senses. When we step into our gardens, we are submerged in sights, smells, sounds, and textures. This is a wake-up call for the part of our brain that processes experience directly and intuitively, instead of categorizing and analyzing it in a detached way. When this part of the brain is stimulated, we tend to become more aware of the sensations and emotions that underlie our busy, rational mind. A garden gives us a chance to remain silent and alone with our feelings, to empty the mind of past and present in order to experience more fully the present moment.'

FROM 'TENDING THE EARTH, MENDING THE SPIRIT: THE HEALING GIFTS OF GARDENING' BY CONNIE GOLDMAN & RICHARD MAHLER HAZELDEN, 2000

Walk Just to Walk

The important thing to consider with walking meditation is that you walk just to walk. Every step you take is a step into the present moment. Try not to focus on your destination. Take each step at a time, and you will soon arrive just where you need to be. If you feel that you are likely to become self-conscious, then I would advise that you try to find a quiet spot in the garden, where you won't be overlooked, as the benefits of slow walking meditation aren't limited by location.

'Walking in mindfulness brings us peace and joy, and makes our life real. Why rush? Our final destination will only be the cemetery. Why not walk in the direction of life, enjoying peace in every moment with every step? There is no need to struggle. Enjoy every step you make. Every step brings you home to the here and the now. This is your true home – because only in this moment, in this place, can life be possible. We have arrived.'

FROM 'HAPPINESS' BY THICH NHAT HANH
PARALLAX PRESS, 2009

EXERCISE 3

A WALKING MEDITATION

• So, find your spot, and stand still, facing the way you wish to walk. Be conscious of the ground beneath your feet, of the sky above your head, and any sensation of the air on your body and clothing.

• Become aware of your breathing. When you breathe in, be aware that you are breathing in. When you breathe out, be aware that you are breathing out. Feel your abdomen rising and falling with each cycle of the breath. Do not force your breath, just let it be in its own rhythm.

• When you are ready begin your walking meditation by breathing in as you take a step with your left foot, and breathe out as you step with your right foot:

Left foot … inbreath

Right foot … outbreath

• As you do this, mindfully observe the sensation of your feet touching the ground, and the feeling of your weight shifting as you walk.

• Sometimes you may feel a bit unsteady on your feet, at least at first, and I have found that if I split my focus to include my trailing leg, then balance is soon restored, and the walking becomes smoother.

• You may find at first that it is easier if you keep your gaze on the ground as you walk. This is fine, especially if the path is uneven.

• Later you may feel confident enough to look at the garden around you. If you do so, try not to allow the mind to start wandering off on its own. Keep it focused on your own wandering!

• The length of time you spend doing this exercise is up to you. Remember it's the quality of your steps, not the quantity, that's important.

• When you feel ready, stop.

• Continue to follow your breathing.

• Relax.

Sometimes it may not be appropriate to take only one step per breath, so feel free to experiment with your own rhythm. If you wanted to take this exercise out onto the streets you may find that three or four steps per breath are right for you, especially if you felt that walking slowly would only serve to draw unwanted attention. Whatever you decide, walking meditation is a simple technique to help you feel calm and relaxed, and in a garden situation is a great way for bringing meditation into action.

WEEDER'S DIGEST

◆

The Earth is a modest planet, who hates to be unclothed. In nature, usually the only time she reveals her bare body is after forest fires, or earthquakes, and even then she soon clothes herself again with pioneer plants to restore her green mantle.

IN THE GARDEN WE CALL THESE PIONEER PLANTS 'WEEDS', and do all we can to eradicate them from our precious plots. Mostly, of course, this is understandable because we have plans to cover the soil with our own chosen pioneers (or should we say 'settlers'?). Despite all this, I admire the plants we so disparagingly term 'weeds'. There is something about their stubborn determination to insist on choosing their own place to live, in spite of our efforts to discourage them, that I find quite appealing. After all, surely they are simply responding to the Earth's plea to cover her modesty, and who are we to question the motives of our own planet!

Learning to Love your Inner Weeds...

As Thich Nhat Hanh says (see box below), we have to learn to love our own inner weeds, those parts of ourselves that we wish weren't there, and which we are forever trying to pluck out. Until we can accept their presence in our psyche, and value them for what they are, they will keep persisting, and

'In Buddhist psychology we say that we are gardeners of our depth consciousness and what we water in ourselves is what grows into this world. There are already some trees and flowers and fruits in our garden. There may be some weeds too. The gardener does not hate the weeds. The good gardener knows how to use the weeds to fertilize the fruit and flowers. The practice of mindfulness does not mean hating the imperfections in ourselves. The practice is to attend to what causes us pain and suffering and use it as fertilizer to create the most beautiful garden possible.'

FROM 'TOGETHER WE ARE ONE' BY THICH NHAT HANH
PARALLAX PRESS, 2010

continue to knock on our door of mindfulness. If we can learn to recognize them as simply a part of our human inheritance, and that they can actually help us to transcend our limited notions of ourselves, the more we can accept our limitations as tools for growth, and not try to deny their existence as seeds in our unconscious mind. We can choose to water those seeds or not, the choice is ours, but we should not turn our backs on them, and pretend they are not there, for they are part of what makes us human, and that is a precious heritage indeed.

...And your Outer Ones, Too

So, whenever you find yourself kneeling in the garden, trowel in hand, ready to rip out those 'perennial nightmares', spare a thought for the qualities of these particular plants, which make them such dogged colonizers of the soil. Regard your battle with them as if it were a game you play together, and that there are no hard feelings whoever wins or loses. Accept the fact that they are not deliberately trying to cause you ill will. They are just being themselves, as much a part of the natural world as are you. Learn to love your so-called 'enemies', however much pain you think they cause you. If you can approach your weeding in this manner, then instead of it being a battle of toil and sweat, accompanied by various expletives at these individual plants, you can help to recognize some of the benefits they may bring you, such as learning patience, persistence and determination!

FLOWER POWER

◆

'You and your activity already exist together in the
realm of emptiness; you are not separate from each other.
When you see yourself, your activity, and your body and mind
in the realm of emptiness, occupying the whole universe, there
is oneness. A beautiful flower is blooming. But there is no way
to discuss that beautiful flower because it is beyond human
speculation, concepts, or ideas. All you can do is pay careful
attention to the reality of that flower as it really is.'

FROM 'EACH MOMENT IS THE UNIVERSE:
ZEN AND THE WAY OF BEING TIME' BY DAININ KATAGIRI
SHAMBHALA PUBLICATIONS, 2007

◆

*Nothing sums up an image of the summer months more than that of
borders packed with flowers. Who does not love them? Their many
forms and colours thrill the eye – and their smell is heaven scent.*

To saunter slowly through a traditional country
garden in its prime is sheer paradise. The kaleidoscope
of colours delights the senses in so many ways, and flower-
filled gardens are simply one of the most exquisite images of
horticultural splendour and abundance.

Flowers play such a huge part in our folklore and history.
They grace our imagination and inspire our poets. They link
us with our ancestors, and offer us their gifts of healing. It's
almost impossible to imagine a world without them.

Our Perception of Colour

The human eye delights in colour, and flowers provide ample opportunity to revel in the richness of hues on offer in all their kaleidoscopic glory. Just to stare deeply into the velvet shades of purple of a tiny viola can be as powerful an experience as gazing intently at the centre of a mandala, as a trigger to a meditative state of mind.

However, we must be mindful of the fact that our sense of vision is limited to only a narrow band of vibration within the spectrum, and the colours as we perceive them are not necessarily real, in a definitive and absolute sense. Bees, and many insects, have a much broader visionary perception, being able to see into the ultraviolet end of the spectrum. For instance, have you ever wondered, in the early spring, why so many bulbous plants are yellow? The bee is very attracted to those flowers, but actually perceives them as rich shades of purple. So which is the 'right' colour? We say a daffodil is yellow, but it is only relatively true. It is not an absolute truth.

What is a Flower?

Botanically, of course, a flower is simply the sexual organ of a plant, designed to tempt pollinators with its alluring charm and promise of sweet nectar, in exchange for which the lucky insect gets, unwittingly, to transfer the vital pollen grains from plant to plant, therefore triggering the genesis of a whole new generation.

The Nature of 'Non-Self'

For anything to manifest, there is an infinite number of factors involved, and for a particular flower you would require: the light and heat from the sun; the whole water cycle leading from the oceans to the clouds and rain, and back again; the gardener who planted it, plus all of his or her life history leading up to the planting; all of the flower's genetic predecessors; the soil within which it grew; the nutrients that helped it to flourish; the bee that provided the pollen to its parent plants; and on and on, ad infinitum. If you were to attempt to factor in all of the connections leading to the manifestation of that flower at that time, you would have to include the entire universe, because of the workings of what Buddhism calls 'interdependent co-arising' or 'dependent origination'. What you will fail to discover is an independent self called 'flower'. This is the nature of 'non-self'. The same is true for us. We are only here because the rest of the universe is here.

'A flower manifests, then disappears, then manifests, then disappears, thousands upon thousands of times. If you look deeply at things, you will see this reality. We manifest, then disappear. It is a game of hide and seek.'

FROM 'YOU ARE HERE' BY THICH NHAT HANH
SHAMBHALA PRESS, 2009

SUFFERING, AND THE WEB OF LIFE

◆

As we know, there are a myriad of creatures, seen and unseen, for which the garden is home. We must learn to respect this, and not lord it over these so-called lesser creatures just because we happen to be in possession of a more complex consciousness.

ADMITTEDLY, THERE WILL BE TIMES when we have to make decisions about how to deal with some of these creatures when there's a danger of them threatening our favoured flowers and shrubs, or endangering our lovingly tended and eagerly awaited crops. Indeed, some gardeners resort to countermeasures at the proverbial drop of a hat after the merest hint of pest damage, only too eager to employ anything, however dubious, from the huge arsenal the horticultural industry has on offer.

Such an approach, I feel, is often misguided, and stems from a belief system that separates the garden from the gardener, rather than a more holistic vision of interconnectedness. There are ways of garden practice that are inclusive of all the species that inhabit 'our' gardens, and can lead to a much more profound and compassionate relationship with our little patch of earth.

This compassion, allied to the wisdom of common sense should be our guideline when deciding how best to deal with pests and diseases.

'Gardening affords us a deep appreciation for
the continuity of nature's seasons and cycles as well
as an understanding of the interconnectedness of all
living beings. Our souls are enriched in the garden
by the business of helping create new life, even when
things look bleak and hopeless. We come to a greater
acceptance of birth, disease, and death because these
are constantly being presented to us. There is an
appreciation of nature's infinite beauty and intrinsic
rhythms as well. We are humbled by our gardens
because they teach us that nature has its own plan,
which includes us. This design is more diverse and
complex than we can ever hope to understand.'

FROM 'TENDING THE EARTH, MENDING THE SPIRIT: THE HEALING
GIFTS OF GARDENING' BY CONNIE GOLDMAN & RICHARD MAHLER
HAZELDEN, 2000

Love is the Best Fertilizer

Plants respond to attention, and if that attention considers
their needs then they can only thrive. It is my firm belief that
love is the best fertilizer, and if we can learn to care for our
green cousins with tenderness they will be far more able to
shrug off any threat from so-called pests. Pests and diseases
are known to be attracted to vibrations, and when a plant is
lacking something, be that enough moisture or nutrients,

they are much more open to attack. So see to the needs of the plants in your care, check what it is they require for optimum health, give them informed wise attention, and there will be far less need to reach for those pellets and sprays.

In Defence of the Slug

Top of most gardeners' lists of reviled pests is no doubt the slug, and its near cousin, the snail. There are, indeed, few of us who have not suffered their ravages at some time or another, and often it has driven us to desperate measures. However, what many people are perhaps not aware of is that in Britain, at least, there are twenty-five species of slug, yet only five or six can be considered a danger to plants. Indeed, the really big slugs actually eat other slugs! So please do not tar all of them with the same brush (even though that may actually sound an effective way to deal with them!). The rest mostly dine on decaying plant material, as well as providing a juicy, if some-what slimy, morsel for the likes of hedgehogs and thrushes.

A Predator's Paradise

This happily brings me to another method to detract pests, and that is biodiversity. A garden packed with a large variety of different species, and where there is a willingness to pro-vide as many habitats for predators as possible, will have few problems. For instance, one of the principal predators of slugs is the ground beetle, which comes out at night in search of prey. By providing areas of long grass, which would eventually form tussocks, you will be providing a perfect place for them to live, and in return they will reward you with munching through your local mollusc population. There are many books these days on the subject of habitat creation and biological control and I would urge you to consider adopting such measures in order to achieve a natural balance within your own particular garden ecosystem.

I feel very strongly that we must get away from this notion of our gardens being under some sort of 'attack'. Very often retailers of pesticides and herbicides use military terms to promote their products, talking about 'wars' and 'battles' against these fiendish creatures and evil weeds waiting in ambush to pounce on the unsuspecting crop or garden plant.

Just Beings 'Being'

We have to change the way we relate to these organisms, and redefine our role as guardians and stewards of 'our' patch of earth. The mindful gardener knows that the likes of bindweed, ground elder, nettles, lily beetles, vine weevils or slugs are simply doing what they're supposed to do. They don't get together like co-conspirators, and then set about scheming how to disrupt our best-laid horticultural plans, firm in the knowledge that they are sworn enemies of all who dare pick up a trowel or spade and venture out into 'their' territory. They are just beings 'being', and so are we.

> 'As Slug, I go through life slowly, keeping close to
> the ground. I offer you just that, humans. You go too
> far, too fast for anyone's good. Know carefully and
> closely the ground you travel on...
>
> I offer you our power as weeds – that of tenacity.
> However hard the ground, we don't give up! We know
> how to keep at it, slowly at first, resting when needed,
> keeping on – until suddenly – crack! And we're in the
> sunlight again. We keep on growing wherever we are.
> This is what we share with you – our persistence.'
>
> FROM 'THINKING LIKE A MOUNTAIN: TOWARDS A COUNCIL OF
> ALL BEINGS' BY JOHN SEED, JOANNA MACY, PAT FLEMING & ARNE NAESS
> HERETIC BOOKS, 1988

Copper Magic

Mention of 'trowels' reminds me that I cannot let this subject
go before letting you know of another method of deterring
our mollusc cousins, which I have successfully utilized for
several years and can recommend wholeheartedly, and that is
the use of copper tools. These wonderful implements have
been available in Britain for a while now, imported by an
English company based in the Midlands (for further information see www.implementations.co.uk).

I first heard about them when reading books about the Aus-
trian forester, philosopher and inventor Viktor Schauberger.

He believed that the use of iron tools was damaging to the earth, and deleterious for plant growth. It is beyond the scope of this book to dwell too long on his reasoning behind this theory, and I would therefore urge you to learn more about this remarkable visionary by checking out the many books and websites concerning his life and work. He had much more faith in the power of copper. When tools are fashioned from this substance (in the form of bronze, i.e. ninety per cent copper and ten per cent tin) they are not only a joy to use, but are also very effective against slugs and snails. I can certainly vouch for the truth of this from my own experience.

It Works

I had already ordered my first copper trowel, and was eagerly awaiting delivery. One day, at work, I had about a hundred marigolds to plant, and proceeded to do so using my usual steel trowel. The next morning, after a particularly wet night, I went to check on them, knowing full well that, along with the likes of lettuce and delphinium, they were pretty much at the top of the menu for slugs. As expected, the slimy ones had had a nocturnal feast and managed to polish off all bar one or two. It just so happened that later that morning I took delivery of my shiny new copper trowel, looking more golden than bronze, and I promptly put it to the test by planting roughly the same amount of marigolds as I had done the previous day, and in the same place. The next morning I returned to the scene of the crime, and to my amazement there was hardly any damage to the flowers, even though it had also been rainy the night before. Since that day I have hardly picked up an ordinary iron-based trowel, and have since added several more copper tools to my arsenal.

Why it Works

If you use a steel trowel, the iron causes an electromagnetic disturbance in the soil area while planting. Copper, it seems, is attracted to such disturbances, and because slugs and snails have copper-based blood they are compelled to head towards them. When they arrive at the area of disturbed soil, they proceed to eat (thus repairing the breakage in the electromagnetic field). By using copper tools there is no disturbance, and therefore no slugs. It sounds like magic, and it is! There are many other positive reasons for using copper tools, which I haven't the space to relate in detail, so I would reiterate that if further information is required, check it out on the internet or by perusing related literature.

Compassion in the Garden

In this world we cannot expect to achieve a 'perfect' garden; no such place exists. As the Buddhist first noble truth proclaims, 'in the world there is suffering'. We have to accept this uncomfortable fact of life. All creatures seek well-being and happiness, a safe world in which to rear their young, and a future free from fear. This is true whether we are human beings or woodlice.

When we have put lots of love and care into growing crops for our families to eat, or filled our gardens with flowers to delight our senses, and we suffer from the attentions of pests and diseases it is definitely heartbreaking, and we often find ourselves swearing vengeance on the culprits (I have certainly done so myself). It isn't wrong to feel this way; it's quite understandable. However, sometimes the better option is to accept what has happened, and look at ways to prevent it reoccurring, without stirring up anger towards what are in truth innocent parties who really only wanted a quick bite to eat!

> 'As a bee gathering nectar does not harm or
> disturb the colour and the fragrance of the flower;
> so do the wise move through the world.'
>
> FROM 'A DHAMMAPADA FOR CONTEMPLATION',
> TRANSLATED BY AJAHN MUNINDO
> ARUNA PUBLICATIONS, 2006

TAKING TIME TO BE STILL

◆

In the ornamental garden, the floral display peaks as the later spring flowers merge with those of early summer, and the roses begin their heady display of scent and colour to draw irresistibly the nose of anyone passing by. This time of year, if the weather proves fair, can be the epitome of summer daze.

JUNE, IN BRITAIN, can be either a gloriously hot month, or just a damp disappointment. Its name derives from the supreme Roman goddess Juno, wife of Jupiter, king of the gods. I believe that the etymology of her name means 'deific light', and considering that her eponymous month includes the summer solstice, I suppose it was well placed in the calendar. That is, depending on whether the sun does actually shine (British skies not having the azure clarity of Italy in June!).

Down Tools and Simply Be

It is so easy at this time of year to do too much, and forget to stop and just enjoy the garden in all its glory. I am guilty of that myself, and I often have to remind myself that it's OK to put down my trowel or hoe, and sit down somewhere quiet, to rest a while, and simply be.

Sit down somewhere quiet to rest a while.

EXERCISE 4

A PLANT MEDITATION

• On entering the garden, walk right up to the plant that attracts you the most, and go and sit in front of it.

• Centre yourself by mindfully following your breath.

• Take as long a time as you like to look closely at the plant – at its shape and form, the nuances and shade of its colouring; look at the way it moves in the breeze, the way it flutters its leaves; notice any insect, or other creature, that may be crawling around on it, or near it.

• Imagine being one of those creatures; how big the plant must appear to it.

• Focus your vision and mind really closely upon it so that its stark existence is laid bare, and observe how it is truly the centre of its own universe. And then…

• Open out your awareness to the rest of the immediate garden surrounding your chosen plant by gradually widening your circle of vision, and it will become very clear to you just what an amazingly vibrant world a garden is, and perhaps give you a real experience of connection, not just with your favoured plant, but with all the myriad forms of life that abound around the garden, and indeed the whole land.

I feel that we need to remind ourselves that we are actually called human 'beings', not human 'doings'. The work ethic engrained in us by our society can often make us feel guilty if we're not always busy. It is an indoctrination hard to shake off, so powerful is its grip on our consciousness. This is highlighted by reversing a well-known phrase, 'don't just do something, sit there', and observing how odd that sounds.

Mindful Pottering

Of course, many people regard 'pottering in the garden' as a way to relax after a busy day at work, or at weekends. For some it is a chance just to unwind after the demands of the day have taken their toll; and for others there is a recognition that here is an opportunity to tune in to natural rhythms, and experience time as cyclic, and not linear, as the world 'out there' would have us believe.

One of the most effective ways of bringing an inner stillness to the practice of pottering is by bringing attention to the present moment in all that you do.

EXERCISE 5

ATTENTION TO STILLNESS

• So start first by connecting with the breath, focusing your awareness on the area just below your navel. Feel the abdomen rising on the inbreath, and falling on the outbreath. Witness the sensation of air entering and exiting your nostrils. Try not to influence the breath, just observe its rhythm. It will naturally slow down by itself.

- Whatever physical action you undertake in the garden, try to follow it closely, while simultaneously maintaining awareness of your breath. When reaching for tools, try to notice when your intention to do so arises, and be conscious of your posture as you stretch out to pick them up. Practise walking meditation as you move around the garden, being attentive to every step. Take your time.

- Be aware of any sounds around, such as birds singing, the rustling of leaves, cries of children, music playing, the noise of traffic, your neighbour's lawnmower, the sounds you, yourself, are making – try not to judge or analyze them. Just let them be.

- Attend closely to any task you undertake, while still paying attention to the rhythm of your breathing and your posture. If you need to slow down those actions in order to maintain mindfulness, that's fine. Slow down. We rush far too much anyway!

Remember, it is good to have balance in life. Just because the rest of the world's energy is everywhere doesn't mean yours has to be. Your garden can serve as a precious sanctuary from the frenetic pace of modern life. Regard it as such, and you will have an effective remedy just beyond your doorstep.

THE JULY GAP

◆

'We live within a belief system that views space and time as
inherently empty containers and sees within that emptiness various
objects move according to deterministic laws. These objects
include animals, plants, and our own bodies. We are led to believe
all objects are fundamentally separate, deriving their existence
and inherent characteristics from their own matter, internal
structure, and organization. Interactions with other objects in
their neighbourhood is thus accidental and not necessary to their
inherent definition or to their continuation as separate entities.'

BY JEREMY HAYWARD, FROM 'DHARMA GAIA: A HARVEST OF ESSAYS
IN BUDDHISM AND ECOLOGY', EDITED BY ALLAN HUNT BADINER
PARALLAX PRESS, 1990

◆

*Just as the garden's energies are speeding up, and everything seems
to be taking off, and we may feel that we could be overwhelmed by it
all, there often occurs a curious pause in the proceedings when the
garden can begin to look a little 'flat'.*

DURING THE HEIGHT AND GLORY OF SUMMER there is so
much abundance it's almost exhausting. Almost every
growing thing is eager to please and trying to attract attention. And then… there nearly always appears a phenomenon
often referred to as 'the July gap'. This is a period when most
of the late spring flowers have spent themselves, and the later
summer flowers haven't matured enough to take their place.

Deadheading...

I find that the best way to prepare for this floral hiatus is the practice of deadheading. It is a technique that can provide an excellent opportunity for putting mindfulness into practice.

The vast majority of flowering plants do not just burst into flower all at once, exhausting their energy, and then spend the rest of the season looking listless and worn out. They have strategies to spread their display over a longer period of time, allowing time for energy coming up from the roots to match energy flowing out of their shoots. The buds develop at different rates, usually with the junior ones being located lower down the stems, and the terminal buds being the first to flower. As we saw in the section on pruning, from the plant's point of view this is to insure against potential grazing and damage in the wild. If this happens, the lower buds take up the slack, thereby ensuring that the plant eventually sets seed and gives rise to future generations.

...with Awareness

Deadheading with awareness is a great practice for training the eye, and for tuning into the plant you are focused upon. Some plants are simpler than others, and so it is best to begin with those, if you have them in your garden. A good example is cosmos. This is a flower that, given the deadheading treatment, can often be in bloom from high summer through to the first frosts, so you definitely get just rewards for your efforts.

EXERCISE 6

A DEADHEADING MEDITATION

• So, first of all, stand in front of the plant you wish to work on and bring your awareness to your breath and posture, being conscious of where you are. When you feel centred and calm within yourself, mindfully reach for and pick up your secateurs or scissors, feeling the pressure of them in your hand, and lovingly regard the plant before you. Recognize that there is no separation between you and the plant. This is simply a process in which the two of you are involved. You do not stop at your skin, and the flower does not stop at its stem. There is connection.

• Look at the plant and bring your attention to its spent flower heads. Notice that lower down the stem there are buds waiting to bloom. Cut out the spent stem, just above the junior buds, being conscious that by doing so you are actively directing energy release into them, which will result in further flowering and the formation of fresh buds below them. Often (as in cosmos), you will see that the spent stem is central to two laterals, each harbouring new buds. So simply cut the central one out. Continue this practice until you have attended to them all.

• When you feel satisfied that you have accomplished this practice, gently bow to the flower, and smile.

WATER, THE ELIXIR OF LIFE

◆

We are truly blessed in Britain in that although we often dream of having long, hot, cloudless summers, what we usually end up with is a mixture of sunshine and showers, with the latter often for prolonged periods. This is good!

PLANTS, IN COMMON WITH ALL OTHER FORMS OF LIFE, need water. It is the presence of this essential element that guarantees life – which is why astronomers around the globe regard it as the 'holy grail' in their search for other inhabitable worlds. On planet Earth, luckily, we have an abundance of this precious liquid, and without it we would have a very barren land indeed.

Plants need it for efficient photosynthesis, and for maintaining healthy cells (we can see this when cells lose moisture, as they soon begin to wilt). Also, the principal reason we water plants is not simply to give them a drink, but because they can only take up nutrients in a soluble solution. Without getting too scientific, water and associated nutrients are carried around the plant in its vascular system, consisting of two parallel tubular vessels called the xylem and phloem. Briefly, the xylem transports essential nutrients from the roots to the shoots, and the phloem does the same with sugars and starches produced by photosynthesis, from the leaves down throughout the body of the plant. The way the vascular system works is akin to the way blood is circulated in animals, and for it to operate efficiently it requires plenty of water, especially as it has been estimated that the vast majority of water previously taken up by the root hairs is eventually lost to the air through transpiration from the leaves, and that only a tiny fraction is actually used by the plant.

Less is More

However, saying that plants need plenty of water could easily be misconstrued to infer that it is good practice to be constantly watering your plants, especially on warm days. At the risk of contradicting myself I must advise that this is not the wisest thing to do!

The key to efficient watering of plants is to do so less frequently, but more thoroughly. If hoses or sprinklers are switched on regularly, even daily, then all that will happen is that plants will only form shallow root systems, not bothering to venture deeper. This will inevitably mean that as soon as the top layer of the ground begins to dry out the plants will start to look wilted, thereby encouraging even more watering, and so the pattern continues.

A much better practice is to water far less often, and by soaking the ground rather than just lightly sprinkling. This way the roots will be encouraged to search for the moisture through deeper layers of soil, and in the process create a stronger and more efficient root system much more able to cope with times of drought, as well as resulting in a stronger plant all round. If you mulch with dry organic matter after a soaking this will result in far less moisture loss, and watering times can be minimized even further.

Be Water Conscious

As water is becoming such a precious commodity these days, any excuse to cut down on its use is to be encouraged. For this reason I am not a big fan of hanging baskets and container gardening (although I do recognize that for some people they are the only practicable option). I feel that the undoubtedly colourful, and sometimes beautiful, floral display simply does not justify the copious amounts of water that hanging baskets require daily, especially when you consider just how many of them there are throughout the country, let alone the world. This certainly cannot be termed a sustainable activity by any stretch of the imagination.

It is a good idea to trust your intuition when it comes to the right time to water plants, rather than simply relying on the clock. Do bear in mind as well that just because leaves look wilted it does not necessarily follow that the plant is crying out for water. If it is a particularly hot day it is more likely that it is just conserving its vital energy by protecting itself from excessive transpiration. So, tune into your plants, and try not to jump to conclusions too readily. They are smarter than you think!

THE GARDEN AS SANGHA

◆

'Only a small area of this Earth can be our
homeland during this lifetime. Dwelling mindfully
in a bioregion, caring for it, becoming intimate with
its seasons, its moods, and becoming friends with its
co-dwellers – the plants and animals – requires clear
intent and regular practice. In our ecocentric Sangha,
we appreciate and hasten our self-realization through
the Self-realization of all beings. Practising in our
bioregion, our life affirms all other life.'

BY BILL DEVALL, FROM 'DHARMA GAIA: A HARVEST OF ESSAYS
IN BUDDHISM AND ECOLOGY', EDITED BY ALLAN HUNT BADINER
PARALLAX PRESS, 1990

◆

*A sangha is the third of the so-called 'three jewels' of Buddhist
teaching, the first and second being the Buddha and the Dharma. We
vow to 'take refuge' in them because they are the cornerstone of our
practice, and central to our spiritual life.*

THE WORD 'SANGHA' IS USUALLY TRANSLATED as 'community', and refers to the connection with our fellow
practitioners, both monastic and lay, within our local groups,
and throughout the Buddhist world. We draw great comfort
from this connection, knowing that the sangha will always be
there for us.

I would like to stretch the meaning to include other areas within which we find ourselves, including our own gardens. For a garden is a community, as it consists of countless beings of differing forms and consciousnesses. Being the human element within this sangha, and possessing the most complex and self-aware consciousness, it is surely our role to act as stewards within this community of fellow organisms; to find ways of being of service to our kindred species and to actively enhance the quality of their existence, with the wisdom of interbeing and love as our tools.

'There is a teaching in Buddhist tradition which tells us that each atom of the universe, at one time or another, has been our mother. And that we have been the mother of each atom as well. Each atom has brought us into being, given us life. Each atom has nourished us, and we have done the same for every atom in the never-ending continuous moment we call our lives. To grasp even a little of this teaching makes quite a difference in how we move through the world; seeing what we see and hearing what we hear. It changes our touching and how we touch, our knowing and how we know.'

BY PETER LEVITT, FROM 'DHARMA GAIA: A HARVEST OF ESSAYS IN BUDDHISM AND ECOLOGY', EDITED BY ALLAN HUNT BADINER PARALLAX PRESS, 1990

CHAPTER THREE

AUTUMN

*At first the trees are tinged with yellow or red,
then a few leaves start to fall; the first chilly morning
is felt, the days are noticeably shorter, and there's a
hint of change in the air. The abundant growth of high
summer looks blowsy now, and in the kitchen garden
the harvest gathers pace. This is a magical time of
year when the contrast between light and dark is
most apparent, and there is a richness in the land.
Time to celebrate the bountiful earth.*

ACCEPTING IMPERMANENCE

◆

As the season changes inexorably to autumn, many people find it a depressing thought that the halcyon days of summer are coming to an end, and yearn instead for a year of endless blue skies and blazing sunshine.

I HAVE OFTEN VIEWED SUCH WISTFULNESS as unrealistic and short-sighted. Surely we have to have balance in life, for how can we appreciate warm days without experiencing cold ones? Or dry days without getting wet? More than that, if the sun constantly shone we would have to say goodbye to our lush green fields and abundant vegetation as the merciless heat beat down on the parched earth; as plants withered in the drought, and desert beckoned.

Far better it would be to accept the slow transformation of the seasons as the miracles they truly are, for they teach us that change is the only constant, and the rich tapestry of life would not be possible without this impermanence. Otherwise, how could an acorn turn into an oak tree; tadpole into frog; seed into flower; or embryo into infant, if it wasn't for impermanence? In order for us to grow up we have to let go of being a child. We have to fully recognize that permanence is really an illusion, and that every phenomenon is always in a state of becoming. The universe is continually recreating itself in every moment.

'Look at the example of a corn seed sown in moist
ground. As a result of the right conditions – water, earth,
warmth – the seed sprouts and produces little leaves. That
corn seed is a very beautiful thing, thanks to impermanence.
"If only that seed wouldn't die!" you might feel. But if the
seed did not die, the plant could not grow.
We have to see that what is happening is not the death
of the seed, but the transformation of the seed into
a plant. Can we detect a permanent entity in either
the seed or the plant? No. A permanent entity is not
necessary to make life possible. With time, the little plant
will become a big plant, which will produce flowers and
then ears of corn. Is a self needed to make it possible for
the corn plant to grow and then produce flowers and
fruit? No, and the same is true for us.'

FROM 'YOU ARE HERE' BY THICH NHAT HANH
SHAMBHALA PRESS, 2009

Letting Go

Once this realization takes hold in one's life it feels more and
more like a liberation, and we are free to enjoy each moment
for what it is: fresh, and poignant with possibility. We can let
go of the old, and face what comes with fervour and freedom,
relishing the opportunities proffered in every instant of time.
Cherishing fully each precious moment is to live life richly.

'Nature changes at the speed of life

From moment to moment, so that all,

Bird, leaf and tree seem still, seem real, until

We glimpse the conjuror at play –

A dandelion's evanescent sphere

Created itself, between yesterday and today

Came, was, and is over, while I

Marvel at that unseen geometer's skill

Who builds the transience where we dwell.'

FROM 'LIVING WITH MYSTERY: POEMS' BY KATHLEEN RAINE
GOLGONOOZA PRESS, 1992

KEEPING IN TRIM

◆

One of the many jobs to do in the garden in autumn is to shape shrubs after the rapid growth and flowering of the summer months. This is a task that offers ample opportunity to practise mindfulness.

TIDYING UP SHRUBS HELPS TO TRAIN THE EYE as well as offering the gardener the opportunity to tune into each plant, and thank it for its contribution to the overall look of the garden during the preceding months.

In the Spring chapter (see 'Shaping Up', p15), I wrote about formative pruning of shrubs at the start of spring; well, this is a similar exercise, but more concerned with neatening them and encouraging them to produce even more potential flowering buds for the following year.

However, do bear in mind that this exercise is only for those shrubs that have already flowered in the summer; so be careful not to apply this to autumn or winter flowering shrubs, or you will almost certainly curtail their display. Obviously you can do so once they have performed their party piece, although it is best to refrain in frosty weather, as you may incur damage to exposed cells, and therefore potentially hamper future re-growth.

Some gardeners prefer just to allow shrubs to grow to their own rhythm, and in their own way, without attempting

'Tending our gardens is an outward physical action that unites body, mind, and spirit. It is like breathing. Taking in air brings us energy, and exhaling releases tensions and promotes letting go and trusting in the next breath. The simple rhythm of successive breaths is both life-sustaining and transformational, connecting us to the air, the sky, the heavens.'

FROM 'CULTIVATING SACRED SPACE:
GARDENING FOR THE SOUL' BY ELIZABETH MURRAY
POMEGRANATE, 1997

any shaping or trimming, and that is, of course, all very fine. Sometimes, however, particularly in a larger garden with a broad vista, the combination of formal curved shapes among naturalistic planting can be very attractive to the eye. The contrast between formality and informality can be quite striking, and the aesthetic effect is often very pleasing.

A Plea for Peace

I just want to give a plea to refrain from using power tools if at all possible. I have often referred to myself as an 'acoustic' gardener, in that I usually eschew the use of loud, fossil-fuelled devices to practise my art, much preferring the quieter, and to my mind more skilful, use of hand tools. I would urge the aspiring mindful gardener to do likewise. It may take longer to accomplish the job in hand, but I believe the garden appreciates the more gentle approach.

EXERCISE 7

A SHAPESHIFTING MEDITATION

• As with all acts performed with mindfulness, it is first of all important to focus on the breath.

• Stand in front of the shrub you wish to work upon and bring your awareness to the rhythm of your breathing. Follow your inbreath closely, and then your outbreath. There is no need to slow your breath down deliberately; this will happen naturally.

• Be conscious of your standing posture, that you feel relaxed and without tension. Connect with the earth below your feet, and the sky above your head.

• Slowly, and deliberately, reach for your shears while being aware of the movement of your body as you do so.

• I often like to acknowledge the shrub by gently bowing to it, with palms together (Zen Buddhists will bow to just about anything given the chance!). This is a nice gesture, and helps you to bring it into the focus of your attention, and also marks the fact that the two of you are connected.

• Regard the current form of the shrub closely, and in your mind's eye superimpose the desired shape you wish to cut to onto that image. I believe that this will alert the devic forces (in this case the nature spirits) to withdraw their energies from the tips of the shrub, which will thereby ensure that the loss of the cut stems is as painless as possible for the organism.

• Holding your shears mindfully, begin trimming the shrub to the shape that you have determined beforehand, and think of yourself as a sculptor slowly and adeptly revealing the form already held within.

• Try not to lose awareness of your breathing, as doing so will help you to maintain your focus, and give a meditative feel to the whole exercise.

• When you have accomplished the task, bow once more to the shrub, and smile to a job well done.

BLOWING IN THE WIND

◆

'Whirled dust, world dust,

Tossed and torn from trees,

No more they labour for life, no more

Shelter of green glade, shade

Of apples under leaf, lifted in air

They soar, no longer leaves…'

FROM 'FALLING LEAVES' BY KATHLEEN RAINE
GOLGONOOZA PRESS, 1993

◆

No gardening task represents autumn as much as the raking of fallen leaves. When you are engaged in it, you just know what season of the year you are in. It is also an excellent way to warm up on a cold and frosty morning, getting the blood flowing and preparing you for further jobs in the garden.

I OFTEN LOVE TO PLAY GAMES WITH THE WIND, especially if there is a breeze blowing, and I rarely mind if I have to go over the same ground twice as the leaves shift and swirl, whirling and spiralling in airy delight. Their fiery reds, warm ambers and crisp browns are a visual treat for the eye, as the ground becomes peppered with kaleidoscopic glitter. They certainly contribute greatly to helping make autumn a memorable season. If you decide to play this game too, see it as a perfect meditation for developing patience!

Why Do Trees Shed their Leaves?

It is worth pausing to consider just why deciduous trees shed their leaves before the onset of winter, because it can help us be more mindful of trees as energetic beings with their own agendas for survival, and through this we can start to appreciate them even more.

> 'Just as there can be logical, clear thoughts that correctly apprehend the phenomena of the physical world, as opposed to illogical, obscure or erroneous thoughts, so there can be living imaginations that apprehend something of the life, soul and spirit of the world. These imaginations must be distinguished from wild and idle fantasies that only confuse and do not explain or point out anything. Logical, discursive thought and imagination are not exclusive; both account for different aspects of the same phenomena.'
>
> FROM 'CULTURE AND HORTICULTURE' BY WOLF STORL
> BIO-DYNAMIC LITERATURE, 1979

It used to be thought that trees shed their leaves simply to conserve their inner processes over the cold winter period, and it was just a question of them switching off chlorophyll production within the individual leaf, revealing the red and yellow pigments beneath the green, then dropping them to the ground, thereby also ceasing evaporation of moisture from the leaves – a good strategy in a season when little or no growth is taking place. Apparently, scientists now believe that what the trees are also doing every year is transferring all of their accumulated toxins and waste materials into the leaves, and then shedding them so that they will be able to decompose gradually into simple elementary particles, thereby purifying the tree each year to start afresh in the spring.

Rake with Awareness

As we rake up the fallen leaves it would be good to acknowledge all of the processes that have gone into them lying there, and that they are not just lying in isolation but are truly linked to all that is around them. Everything is interdependent, and by using our imagination we can create connections between those fallen leaves and the whole

Be mindful of stretching and reaching, and the position of your legs.

of the cosmos. Try to be aware of your posture as you rake, be mindful of stretching and reaching, and the position of your legs. Use your imagination and pretend it's a horticultural version of tai chi!

FLORAL FIREWORKS

◆

When it comes to the planting of spring bulbs, this has to take place in autumn, or there will be no show. Planning the effect can be an exciting exercise, and I often liken the practice to lighting the green touch paper of a particularly colourful firework display, only with a very long fuse!

G ARDENERS ARE WELL KNOWN TO ALWAYS BE LOOKING at least a couple of seasons ahead, and even longer, and although it may seem to go against the Buddhist injunction always to seek to dwell in the present moment, it does have some horticultural merit.

When I plant masses of bulbs I often smile to myself thinking about the visual effect that will manifest in the spring, and the joy it will be for those who see it. When there is a team of gardeners involved in such an enterprise, it is like everyone is taking part in a conspiracy to thrill the senses at some future date. When the bulbs do eventually appear there is then a direct connection between their display and the actions of those gardeners, thereby linking time and space, and it is good to recognize this fact as an example of interbeing. Within the present moment there is no actual separation between the past action and the present result. All phenomena occur only in the here and now. The biggest firework display of all, the Big Bang, is occurring in every moment.

Think Deep

Most bulbs can happily be left in the ground to multiply slowly over time, although it is worth considering a few pointers to assure success. One thing that is very important is to bury them to the correct depth, otherwise there is the chance that they will dry out and be unable to perform. The usual recommendation is to plant them at least twice their length. One other advantage to burying them deep is that they are less likely to be disturbed by a plunging trowel whenever you need to plant other species in the same area.

Be Adventurous

Being someone who likes to be adventurous when planting bulbs, I would encourage you to pay that little bit extra and plant more uncommon varieties. Tulips, daffodils, crocuses (or should that be 'croci'?) and hyacinths are all very well, but they are not all that is on offer. Browsing catalogues is an activity that the majority of gardeners love to do, sparking off, as it inevitably does, thoughts and ideas for future planting schemes. Often the sheer volume of bulbs on offer can be quite daunting, and I suppose it is understandable that a lot of gardeners opt for the tried and tested varieties with which they are familiar. I would urge you to break that habit.

Without going into detail about their individual merits, here is a short list of the more unusual, or less familiar, bulbs that you might want to consider planting: triteleia, sparaxis, ixia, hermodactylus, chionodoxa, Anemone coronaria, nectaroscordum, erythronium, dwarf irises (especially the wonderful 'Katherine Hodgkin'), dodecatheon, ipheion, Allium schubertii and Allium christophii.

> 'Just as the creation of a garden is a
> continuous process going on through the
> years, so the enjoyment of it grows with time.
> The original idea grows with the thought given to
> it by its owners and their friends and develops into
> a more elaborate realization of the first vision;
> it becomes a part of the culture of the day.
> In contemplation of it we enlarge our vision with
> the perspective of other cultures while at the same
> time drawing on the eternal source of
> our existence in nature.'
>
> FROM 'THE MYSTIC GARDEN' BY DOUGLAS SWINSCROW
> THE HALSGROVE PRESS, 1992

That should be enough to be getting on with! I have grown all of the above in the past, and present, and can thoroughly recommend them. These bulbs hail from various parts of the globe, and by growing them in your garden you will be linking in with other countries and helping to connect, albeit in a small way, with other cultures. In fact the majority of our plants come from overseas, thanks mostly to the efforts of Victorian plant hunters, and our gardens are a veritable United Nations flying the flag for horticultural unity. This can only be a good thing – so don't simply plump for the familiar, bring a little exotica into your life!

THE WAY OF MULCH

◆

'Energy is indeed present in all things. Living organisms draw it from their environment, as plants take it from the sun in photosynthesis and animals take chemical energy from their food through digestion and respiration. They accumulate it in their own bodies and use it to power their movements and behaviour. When they die, the energy accumulated in their bodies is released to continue on its way in other forms. The flow of energy on which your body and your brain depend at this very moment is part of the cosmic flux, and the energy within you will flow on after you are dead and gone, taking endless new forms.'

FROM 'THE REBIRTH OF NATURE: THE GREENING
OF SCIENCE AND GOD' BY RUPERT SHELDRAKE
PARK STREET PRESS, 1994

◆

A mulch (a delightful Old English word meaning 'soft') is the term given to any organic material applied to the surface of soil and incorporated back into the ground by the action of earthworms.

As I said earlier, I am not a fan of digging, i.e. inverting the soil with a spade. This practice only serves to disrupt the ecology of the soil organisms and minerals, and then you have to wait a period of time before balance is restored. A much better way to work the soil is to apply a mulch.

The optimum organic material is anything that has a fair amount of fertility within it, such as homemade compost or well-rotted manure, although practically anything will suffice as long as it is non-synthetic. However, be warned not to assume that this applies to freshly cut plants or raw foodstuffs, as the bacteria that would be triggered into breaking down the material may initially utilize too much nitrogen from the soil, and this may potentially affect the growth of plants within the mulched area.

Why Mulch?

There are many benefits to laying down an annual mulch, not just the fact that after a few years of regular application you will inevitably end up with a soil possessing an excellent structure and tilth – easily worked and a joy to cultivate. Other benefits include:

• preventing evaporation of moisture from the ground, thereby protecting the roots from drying out;

• insulating the soil during cold periods;

• suppressing the germination of weed seeds through the blockage of light, thereby saving labour;

• encouraging worm activity, which helps to aerate the soil particles, making it more easily workable;

• slowly releasing nutrients as it breaks down, which encourages good growth for subsequent plants;

• helps prevent soil compaction after bouts of prolonged heavy rain;

• and finally, there is an aesthetic consideration as mulches also look good, providing a dark and attractive backdrop for any plants growing within it.

Weed Before Mulching

One thing that mulches will not do is prevent the more persistent perennial weeds such as bindweed, nettles, ground elder, dock, etc. from growing, so it is vital that the mindful gardener is aware of this and takes effective measures to extricate them as thoroughly as possible before applying a mulch. Saying all that, however, it is true that after a number of years of regular mulching these perennial weeds are much more easily dug up, should they seed themselves around, due to the increased depth of easily worked soil, i.e. tilth (another wonderful Old English word!)

Mulches will not prevent the more persistent perennial weeds.

NATURE'S BOUNTY

'Earth brings us into life and nourishes us.

Countless as the grains of sand

in the River Ganges,

all births and deaths are present in each breath.'

AN EXTRACT FROM 'EARTH GATHAS' BY THICH NHAT HANH,
FEATURED IN 'DHARMA GAIA: A HARVEST OF ESSAYS IN BUDDHISM
AND ECOLOGY', EDITED BY ALLAN HUNT BADINER
PARALLAX PRESS, 1990

As autumn progresses, more and more plants reach their annual zenith by successfully producing seed and berry, thereby ensuring the continuance of future generations. This is the season when we humans, plus all the other animals, can feast on, and celebrate, nature's fruitful abundance.

WHEN THE URGENCY OF GROWTH BEGINS TO DIMINISH, the parent plant often then begins the process of withdrawing its energies in preparation for the slumber of winter, either by directing energy into preparing for next year's buds and shoots, or by self-sowing around its base before yielding to the cold embrace of the early frosts.

This is a busy time for wildlife, as birds feast on juicy berries, bees and butterflies gorge themselves on sweet nectar, and squirrels frantically bury nuts with the hope that they will remember where they are come the darker days of winter.

Reaping the Rewards

For kitchen gardeners and allotment holders, this is the time of year when we are rewarded by the fruits of our labours as we reap our harvest of plenty. There is nothing more satisfying than filling your plate and belly with food you have grown yourself. It makes all the trials and tribulations of the gardening year worth the time and physical effort, and can be very life-affirming.

It is no wonder that throughout human history people have marked harvest time with great celebrations and rituals. It was, and still is in many cultures, the most significant time of year, bonding the tribe with the land, and offering to people outward proof of the bountifulness of Mother Nature.

Being Grateful

This is a good opportunity for us to give thanks for all that we have harvested in the current year, both internally and externally. To recognize, even when we are in the midst of struggling to cope with the exigencies of life, that we will get our rewards; we will some day reap benefit for our effort and persistence. Often when we find ourselves in difficult situations we may not imagine that there can possibly be a light at the end of the proverbial tunnel; however nothing, and no situation, lasts forever. All is constantly in a state of becoming. If we can fully grasp this truth, then we will be able to cope with anything life may throw at us. When we do finally reap our rewards, it is natural to want to celebrate it. We have buried deep within us ancestral seeds linking us to our fore-bears, and given that we are only a mere hundred generations since the Iron Age, it is no wonder that we feel it so strongly. In this modern, so-called sophisticated age we would do well to water these seeds, and reawaken our link with our ances-tors. They are closer to us than we may think.

EXERCISE 8

AN ANCESTRAL MEDITATION ON ABUNDANCE

• Gather together various natural items, such as seeds, berries, nuts and fruits which symbolize harvest and fulfilment.

• Find a spot in the garden, where you can sit on the ground with these specimens arrayed in front of you as a makeshift altar. Add any extra seasonal offerings like fallen leaves and fungi, and perhaps a bowl, or other receptacle, to symbolize reaping and gathering.

• Be aware of the presence of other creatures around you, who in their own way may be celebrating their own particular harvest. Sense your kinship with them.

• Look closely at these items, taking time to dwell on each one. See them not just as the culmination of the cycle of growth, but also as its continuation. Give thanks to the Earth, for all of her gifts.

• Now close your eyes, and bring your awareness to your

breath, follow its rhythm with attention. Be aware too of your posture, and of the solidity of the ground upon which you sit.

• Listen closely to any sounds you may hear, beginning with the loudest, and gradually focusing on the quietest. Sense the presence of the living, vibrant world all around you.

• Imagine yourself as one of your ancestors giving thanks to the Earth for her abundance. Go further and further back in time, in your mind, to the earliest days of humanity on this precious planet, and connect with the peoples of that land. Recognize that there really is no distance in time and space between you. All of history happens in the flash of the present moment. They live within you, as you live within them. Feel the kinship. Pause a while within this realization.

• When you are ready, and using your breath as an anchor, gradually bring your attention back to your place in the garden, and gently open your eyes.

• Being aware of your body's movements, slowly stand up, and with palms together, bow to your altar in thankfulness, and smile.

Imagine yourself as one of your ancestors giving thanks to the Earth for her abundance.

Frost, the Great Leveller

◆

Frost is another phenomenon associated with this time of year. I have dubbed it 'the great leveller' because a plant's ability to cope with degrees of frost marks it out as either hardy, half-hardy or tender.

SOME PLANTS BARELY SEEM TO NOTICE FROST, while others turn brown immediately upon contact with its icy embrace. On cold clear nights, the cells expand rapidly in the plunging temperature and soon burst their cell walls, and often all you are left with is a very slimy brown 'mush'. Admittedly, not the most pleasant of tasks – anyone who has tidied up dahlias, lettuces or nasturtiums after a hard frost will know just what I mean!

Because cold air is heavier than warm air, gardens at the bottom of a hill can suffer from frost more than those on a slope, especially if there are any physical barriers at the bottom, such as a hedge or wall, which can act like a dam, causing the cold air to back up and form a frost pocket. So the mindful gardener would be unwise to grow frost-tender plants at the bottom of such a slope. If, however, you are determined, then you can always prune out the lower branches of the hedge, thus leaving a gap, which would effectively allow the cold air to flow past, and therefore not form a pocket. The equivalent for a wall would be to have an opening, such as a gateway, which would probably be just as effective.

> 'The cosmos reverberates with divine energies...
>
> To partake in the Divine, your consciousness must be so
> finely tuned that it is divine itself. The great mystery of the
> evolutionary process is that it can produce consciousness
> which is capable of embracing the Divine, by being itself
> an aspect. The closer we come to the Divine the more we
> can experience the Divinity of the Universe.'
>
> FROM 'A SACRED PLACE TO DWELL: LIVING WITH
> REVERENCE UPON THE EARTH' BY HENRYK SKOLIMOWSKI
> ELEMENT BOOKS, 1993

The First Frosts

In times past the gardener's year in the northern hemisphere
would traditionally end at Halloween, also known as Samhain
(the old name for the end of October, beginning of November,
and a time, incidentally, when one would also celebrate one's
ancestors). Perhaps one of the reasons for this could be
because it is at this time of the year that the first frosts would
appear, and its effects would naturally cause the demise of a
lot of plants and crops, thus marking an end to that particular
cycle and the beginning of planning the next.

Despite all the so-called negative effects of frost, I must say
that walking around in it can at the same time be quite exhilarating. There's a fresh crispness to the air, which can make us
feel more alive somehow. The visible coolness of breath and

the sense of cold around one's body can be an immediate way of being fully present in the moment. There are times, especially when out walking on clear and frosty nights, and gazing up at the night sky, when one can feel a real sense of being part of the cosmos. The small self is somehow transcended, and the sense of interconnection with all of life can be profound; and magic is afoot.

PLANTING THE FUTURE

Trees span the breadth of our lives. They can live for several decades, centuries, or even millennia. They link us to our ancestors, and to our descendants. Trees are the most majestic of plants, and loom large in our historical memory and folklore. They are, quite literally, awesome — in their longevity, and in their sheer presence.

THE IMPORTANCE OF TREES to the sustainable maintenance of the planet is immense. They are truly the lungs of the Earth, breathing in vast quantities of carbon dioxide, and breathing out oxygen. Without their contribution to creating, and recreating, our atmosphere, it would be a very different, and difficult, planet on which to live.

I believe everyone ought to take the opportunity to plant at least one large tree in their lives, if not for themselves, at least for future generations. In fact, horticulturally speaking, to do so would be a prime example of a selfless act. For those who have taken the bodhisattva vow, this could be a key practice.

Late autumn is an excellent time for planting trees, as energy takes a rootward shift. Doing so at this time of the year will thus enable the sapling to have plenty of time to get itself settled in before the upward rise of spring, and the emergence of its new leaves.

'O never harm the dreaming world,
The world of green, the world of leaves,
But let its million palms unfold
The adoration of the trees.

It is a love in darkness wrought
Obedient to the unseen sun,
Longer than memory, a thought
Deeper than the graves of time.

The turning spindles of the cells
Weave a slow forest over space,
The dance of love, creation,
Out of time moves not a leaf,
And out of summer, not a blade.'

FROM 'VEGETATION, SELECTED POEMS' BY KATHLEEN RAINE
GOLGONOOZA PRESS, 1993

Location, Location

The first, and most important, consideration has to be its position. Always check its expected fully mature height, and plant accordingly. So many people unwisely decide on completely inappropriate locations (such as next to pathways), and then have to cut the poor tree down because it has outgrown its space. It is crucial that you take full responsibility for the tree's future health and well-being. Given the truth of interbeing, you will be directly connected to the demise of the tree if at some future date it has to be felled due to unskilful planting. Remember that this is a sentient being with a right to grow to its full potential, and the onus is on you to plant it in as optimum a position as possible.

Preparing the Plot

Once the position is sorted out, the next task is digging the hole within which to plant the tree. This has to be wide enough to allow the roots to be splayed out fully, in the case of a bare-root specimen, without bending them, or at least not too much. With container-grown trees, ensure that you always tease out any roots that have curved around the pot, otherwise they may simply continue doing so and the tree may fail to establish itself properly. Common practice is to widen the hole to approximately twice the width of the pot; this will ensure that the roots are able to grow out easily into the surrounding soil.

To Fertilize or Not?

It used to be that gardeners were encouraged to add compost or other organic fertilizers to the hole before placing the tree, but it is now accepted that this may actually be detrimental to firm establishment, the idea being that the tree's roots would simply choose to hang around the immediate vicinity rather than venturing out in search of nourishment, thereby resulting in potential instability and the possibility of being uprooted during stormy weather. It is still a good idea, however, to break up the bottom and sides of the planting hole with a fork, as spades can create a hard pan while sliding through the soil, making it less attractive to roots.

Stake Firmly

A newly planted tree can be affected by strong winds, so it is advised that you stake it well. So as not to damage any roots, it is recommended that the tree is staked after the hole has been dug, and before the displaced soil is put back in. Only a short stake (a quarter of the height) is required, as the stability of the roots, not the trunk, is the reason for using a stake. Trees actually benefit from swaying in the wind, as it makes for a stronger trunk. Always plant the tree at the same depth as the root flare (i.e. where the topmost roots flare out from the trunk), or soil level of the pot. Place the stake at a 45-degree angle from the prevailing wind, and secure to the tree using a proper tree tie and spacer.

Water Well

Gradually fill in the hole with the displaced soil, and firm with a foot (putting weight on the standing foot, so as not to compact the soil too much). Make sure that the tree gets a thorough watering and subsequent soakings until you feel certain it has fully established itself. Trees take up lots of water so do not think it sufficient to give it a mere sprinkling every now and then. It is much better to saturate seldom than to sprinkle often.

Remember, planting a tree is a gift to the future. Your descendants will thank you for it.

INTO THE DARK

◆

Samhain (pronounced 'Sow-ain') is a very crucial and transformative time of year. It marks the ending of one cycle and the beginning of the next. Energy, which has been so active during the summer months, now begins its descent into the darkness of the root zone.

A KEY EXAMPLE OF THIS is that when late autumn arrives we gardeners know that the time has come when we can plant bare-root shrubs and trees, something we would not dream of doing earlier in the year when energy is focused upwards. The shift in energetic direction towards the roots ensures that the shrub will become established come the spring.

As I mentioned earlier, our ancestors are traditionally honoured at this time of year, and is this not an example of our consciousness echoing nature by seeking to connect with our own roots? Is this not proof of the old adage 'as above, so below'? Of microcosm reflecting the macrocosm?

> 'Darkness has been associated with fear and evil in our culture for hundreds of years, but it was not always so. To the Celts and the ancient civilizations, the Dark was celebrated as a place inside us where we touch and experience our spiritual roots and was known as the Mysteries.'
>
> FROM 'THE ALCHEMIST'S JOURNEY: AN OLD SYSTEM
> FOR A NEW AGE' BY GLENNIE KINDRED
> HAY HOUSE, 2005

A Trying Time

For a lot of people this time of the year can be difficult. The long and light days of high summer are well and truly over, and autumn is making way for the short and darkened days of winter. The natural world is marked by death and decay, and we are forced to accept this uncomfortable truth, reluctantly preparing ourselves by gathering our inner energies and withdrawing into the warm comfort of our homes, and staying indoors as much as possible, drawing the curtains on life.

That is, unless you are an active gardener! For there is still plenty to do to keep the blood pumping and our bodies warm. There are the last of the leaves to search out and rake up in all those corners and crevices we earlier overlooked. The compost heap could probably do with its final turn of the year before settling down over the winter; be sure to cover it up during the cold weather as this will keep the friendly bacteria nice and snug, and encourage them to persist a little longer before easing off until the spring – something like an old natural fibre carpet would be perfect.

Any usable leaf mould could be well utilized by placing it around woodland plants such as hellebores and ferns, and any fairly tender plants, as it will help to insulate the surrounding soil from the effects of freezing weather conditions.

Last Trimmings

High winds can be very frequent in late autumn and it is good practice to cut back the likes of roses, buddleia and other woody shrubs by approximately fifty per cent so as to protect them from potential wind rock, which can cause damage to the roots. This will also prepare the plants for their eventual, more formative pruning in the early spring.

It is also very important to take a break from gardening every now and then in order to tune into our more unconscious, intuitive side. Remember, just as nature is slowing down, it's OK for the gardener to do likewise!

EXERCISE 9

CONNECTING TO YOUR ROOTS

• After it has gone dark, preferably on a dry day with a slight breeze blowing, wrap up warm and go and stand in a favourite spot somewhere within the garden.

• Keeping a straight back, consciously connect with your posture, close your eyes, feel your presence in this place.

• Bring your attention to your breath, following closely the process of breathing in... and breathing out... breathing in... and breathing out... Sense your abdomen rising with each inbreath... and falling with each outbreath... rising... falling... rising... falling... Watch this process for a few minutes, and relax.

• Sense the immensity of the sky above you; feel the wind outlining your body with its touch. If you feel cold, try not to tense up, just be with it.

• Feel the energy pouring down through every molecule of your body, to the tips of your fingers, to the soles of your feet.

• Now focus your concentration on the ground beneath your feet, the hard, solid surface supporting your body. Give thanks for this solidity, this firm planet Earth, which has held you for all of your life.

• Visualize this energy slowly sinking down into the roots of the earth, and as you do so bring to mind your own

roots: your birthplace; your parents and grandparents;
the landscape, village, town or city in which you grew up;
any early experiences that were key to making you who you
are now.

• As you look deeply at these images, send love to yourself as
you were then, and try to recognize the patterns of your life
that have led to your present state of being. Feel free to cry if
these memories are tender or painful.

• When you feel ready, slowly bring the energy up from the
ground below to the air above, once again pausing at the place
where your feet touch the earth. Dwell there a moment and
acknowledge that, just as a plant does not consist of just its
top growth, neither do you. The roots of who you are lie in
the 'darkness' of the subconscious, the store consciousness,
which hold the pregnant seeds of your past, present and
future. Which seeds you wish to water to grow into the light
of day is entirely up to you.

• Finally, gently bow to who you were, who you are, and who
you wish to be. And smile!

*The roots of who you are lie in the
'darkness' of the subconscious.*

CHAPTER FOUR

WINTER

Nature strips down to her bare bones;
trees reveal themselves as the lungs they truly are;
gardeners are braced for the full onslaught of wild,
wet and windy weather. Time to wrap up warm
as darker days and dormancy reign. There is often
a brisk breeze and fresh crispness in the air, which
can be exhilarating. Hardy birds and other creatures
scurry about seeking sustenance from frozen berries,
or food scraps put out for them. Life is suspended
pending the return of milder weather.

THE LESSONS OF STARKNESS

◆

'At the back-end of time

Leaf-fall of lives, dwindling of the great tree

To the acorn of forests, returning

To the nothing of all that is,

The seasons, the leaves, the loves,

Song to its source, soul to its star –

Winter's recollection of worlds to be.'

FROM 'LIVING WITH MYSTERY 1987–91' BY KATHLEEN RAINE
GOLGONOOZA PRESS, 1992

◆

Despite it being generally freezing cold, dark and wet (some would say miserable), I actually love the winter. I cherish it for its simplicity as animals and plants withdraw into themselves, either by hibernating in nest and burrow, or by shrinking into the gnomic world of roots. The land is then enabled to pause within its paucity.

THIS SEASON IS A NATURAL AND NECESSARY COUNTERBAL-
ANCE to the frantic, and sometimes frenetic, activity of summer. Without the inbreath of wintertime, the yearly cycle would be unbalanced, and out of kilter with natural law.

We all need time in our lives to rest and take stock, to review the old year and preview and plan for the next. Every inhalation is followed by an exhalation, without it the breath would not be complete. Winter is a good season in which to tune into this rhythm. Nature is only slumbering, she is not comatose; she will awaken as the wheel continues to turn. Winter teaches us patience. The warm days will inevitably return. Until they do, this is a time for gathering around, or in front of, a blazing fire with our friends and families to tell tales and make merry. Times like these, in the past, were key to re-emphasizing the connections between members of the tribe or clan, and helped to strengthen friendship and family bonds. We continue this tradition to the present day when families yield to the strong impulse to come together at Christmas and New Year, as they have always done since times past over the winter solstice period.

THE YIN OF THE YEAR

This is a time to be still, and to reflect; it is the yin of the year. Instead of the mad rush around the garden within which we are whirled during the hectic days of spring and summer, winter offers us the opportunity to slow down, to walk with ease and unhurried intent.

To accomplish our seasonal tasks with a calm mind and peaceful purpose necessitates a more meditative method in the work that we do, and if we can succeed in doing so we will then be more prepared to face the growing exigencies of spring when they do eventually arise.

'Our lives today are governed by the endless ticking
of the clock. The ancients talked of the Wheel of Time,
the constant circle of birth and rebirth. We choose a
totally different metaphor: for us, life is a constantly
flowing stream. In our mind's eye time marches or flies;
it never stands still and it never recedes. This linear view
of time makes us harried and impatient, and is the root
cause of the hurry sickness which has become such a
destructive feature of our modern lives.'

FROM 'THE THERAPEUTIC GARDEN' BY DONALD NORFOLK
BANTAM BOOKS, 2000

For the mindful gardener, winter is a time for taking stock of
what worked and what didn't. With the garden down to a
simpler, less crowded, structure we can see the layout and
design more clearly. This gives us the chance to move things
around, dig up what hasn't worked, and relocate in a more
favoured spot. The key is to slow down and not to rush
around; there is plenty of time.

Letting Winter Simply Be

Nurseries often take advantage of the gardener's urge to plant
by offering tempting deals for winter bedding. This is all well
and good, as these plants can certainly help to brighten up the

brown hues of winter, but I would urge a certain amount of restraint, not to cover every bare patch with floral expectation when a good mulch is all that is needed. I do accept that this is my own prejudice speaking, but as a long time naturalistic gardener I personally prefer gardens to reflect the time of year, and to me, gardens are meant to have gaps in the winter. They are not supposed to and should not be expected to flower away as if it were still the height of summer; barring of course those plants that naturally do wait until the shorter days before displaying their virtues. In the northern hemisphere, the natural world is meant to be stripped bare, and attempts to deny this go against the grain.

Right Tidiness

◆

'Gaia abhors uniformity. She does not attempt to impose homogeneity, but encourages every living thing to develop to achieve fulfilment, in its own individual way. Every leaf, every pebble, every living cell is different from all others. Similarly, human beings, in their relations with the land, its flora and fauna, should strive to promote the diversity which is the truest freedom.'

From 'Beyond the Forest Garden' by Robert A. de J. Hart
Gaia Books, 1996

◆

There are gardeners who abhor untidiness, and are passionate about keeping their gardens or allotments entirely free from anything that might spoil, to their mind, the purity of their precious plot. I wish them well, but I'm not one of them!

I
T'S TRUE THAT THE IMAGE OF NEATLY CUT LAWN EDGES, grass completely free from any weeds that dare to show themselves, neat rows of vegetables, and perfectly symmetrical planting schemes does have a certain aesthetic quality to it, but such displays can often seem a little sterile. I would prescribe a little more looseness on the horticultural front. Taken to an extreme, such obsession can do serious damage to the mind, resulting in what should be a pleasant day's gardening being constantly peppered with rage whenever a nonconformist plant appears to wreck the uniformity, and the hapless gardener feeling forced to respond by bringing out the heavy artillery of herbicidal warfare.

Turning Over an Old Leaf

There is some case for doing a little bit of tidying up in the winter garden, especially if there are still heaps of autumn leaves lying on top of plants. A small amount of leaves is fine on bare patches, as they should eventually be incorporated into the soil by the actions of earthworms and other organisms, but it is not a good idea to leave larger amounts on top of the crowns of over-wintering hardy perennials as this may cause fungal problems, or harbour slugs. It is acceptable to let some leaves remain around the more tender plants, as this will help to insulate them against cold temperatures, especially if the area has not been mulched. Trust your intuition and common sense on how much you leave.

Let It Be

When it comes to old stalks, it depends on whether they are of interest to wildlife; any with seed heads still attached should be left, at least until all of the seeds have been consumed by birds. Hollow stems can provide a snug retreat for insects over the winter, so be mindful of this before you cut them all down. Some stems can be left for architectural interest if they provide attractive features during frosty weather.

Having areas of long grass is always a good idea, especially if the grass is left to form tussocks, as these provide excellent habitat for ground beetles, which are among the gardener's best friends as they are key controllers of the slug population. They venture out at night in search of juicy morsels, so if you can leave at least small parts of the lawn to its own devices the beetles will love you for it!

Practising Good Hygiene

If you have roses, it would be wise to pick up any leaves from plants that have suffered from black spot, as the spores will inevitably survive over winter and lead to re-infection the following year. On the allotment this also applies for any mildewed leaves of soft fruit. The leaves should not be placed on the compost heap for the same reason, and should preferably be burned. With both of these diseases, good hygiene is the key to controlling their spread.

> 'We live within a belief system that views space and time as inherently empty containers and sees within that emptiness various objects move according to deterministic laws. These objects include animals, plants, and our own bodies. We are led to believe all objects are fundamentally separate, deriving their existence and inherent characteristics from their own matter, internal structure, and organization. Interaction with other objects in their neighbourhood is thus accidental and not necessary to their inherent definition or to their continuation as separate entities.'
>
> BY JEREMY HAYWARD, FROM 'DHARMA GAIA: A HARVEST OF ESSAYS IN BUDDHISM AND ECOLOGY', EDITED BY ALLAN HUNT BADINER
> PARALLAX PRESS, 1990

Any prunings, or fallen twigs, can also be placed on a bonfire, as not only is this a great way to get warm on a chilly day, but also the ash can then be deposited onto the compost heap.

TOOLS FOR GROWTH

◆

*Where would humans be without tools? Apart from a few instances
(such as when thrushes utilize stones to break open snail shells, or
monkeys use sticks to reach for honey), the use of tools is what marks
us apart from other animal species.*

P ROBABLY THIS IS DUE NOT ONLY TO OUR SELF-AWARENESS
and greater intellectual capacity for problem solving, but
also because we possess opposing thumbs. This gives us great
dexterity to hold and utilize implements with our hands.
Indeed the word 'technology' derives from a Greek word
meaning 'art or craft', implying the use of our hands.

For the gardener, tools are crucial. We probably could
manage without them but our hands would inevitably end up
extremely rough and calloused, no doubt with innumerable
cuts and bruises. I would imagine if that were the case there
would be few takers for a course in horticulture!

TLC for Tools

Given their importance, it is very clear that it is our duty to
look after our garden tools and keep them in good shape.
Winter is an excellent season to give them some attention,
especially on really wet and windy days, which are very
common at this time of the year, and there is not much else
that one can do, certainly not outside in the garden itself.

This is definitely an excuse for ensconcing yourself in the shed, or utility room, with a cup of hot tea, and all the various accoutrements necessary to give a bit of mindful attention to all of the tools that help you fulfil your horticultural endeavours. What you need is a selection of various cloths, a wire brush or steel wool, perhaps an old toothbrush for the fiddly jobs, and a bottle or two of linseed oil (boiled or raw).

Implementation Contemplation

I think it is a good exercise to spread out all of your tools in front of you and simply regard them. By that, I mean to look at each of them one at a time and contemplate your use of them, perhaps bringing to mind instances when you have used them; thinking back through the previous year, and picturing yourself with them in your hand. As your attention moves from one to the other, give thanks to each one of them, see them as an extension of your hands (which they are); give a little bow or nod to them, if you wish, as a ritual of acknowledgement of their part in your gardening life. Contemplate the truth that they and you are one.

The Cleaning Ritual

The first thing to do is to ensure that the tools are clean, so scrub them and dry them well. Use the wire brush if any of the metal is becoming rusty; then wipe them over with an oily rag. This will help to protect from future decay. A regular application of oil throughout the year would be of great benefit to prolonging tool life expectancy. It is worth noting that copper tools do not rust – another good reason for considering purchasing them. Turning your attention now to the handle (assuming it is made of wood), and first checking that it is clean, proceed to rub in the linseed oil with a clean cloth or brush, ensuring that the whole surface is covered. Linseed is a versatile oil derived from the flax plant, and has been used for centuries for preserving wood from decay. Leave to dry thoroughly before using again.

WINTER SOLSTICE, THE PAUSE BETWEEN BREATHS

'The Earth has been withdrawn inside herself.
Winter brings the hardships of cold and shortness of daylight. Very little growth has happened, but deep within the Earth, roots have been growing, bringing stability and nutrients to the plants and trees. New buds are slowly forming on the trees and bushes and deeply buried bulbs are beginning to send up their first hardy shoots. All of nature has slowed down, waiting for the energy to change and for warmth to return.'

FROM 'SACRED CELEBRATIONS: A SOURCEBOOK' BY GLENNIE KINDRED
GOTHIC IMAGE, 2004

While observing the rhythm of the breath in meditation there appears to be a noticeable brief pause between the ending of the exhalation and the beginning of the inhalation. The solstices are often seen as equivalent phenomena within the rhythm of the Earth's annual cycle.

THEY ARE KEY POINTS within the dance of the seasons, marking as they do the times in the year when the sun appears to rise at its most northerly and southerly latitudes, i.e. the tropics of Capricorn and Cancer, respectively.

Celebrating these times of year has been a part of our history for millennia, and for many cultures, in either hemisphere, they are of the greatest significance. Indeed there has been a massive upsurge in support for these ancient festivals in recent times as people everywhere seek a deeper connection with the planet upon which they live.

The winter solstice marks the darkest time of the year, when the nights are at their longest, and the days seem so brief. This is a time of great power, the darkness drawing us inwards, deep within our psyche.

A Time to be Still

This can be a great opportunity for us too to pause, to take a break from the rush of the everyday, and simply be. Not in order to judge ourselves and our lives, but rather just to sit quietly, not expecting anything, just breathing, stilling our mind, calm and at peace. If you can consult an ephemeris (which lists the astrological positions of the planets for each year), or check online for when the sun enters the sign of Capricorn, then this meditation will have more meaning and authenticity, although any time close to the solstice point would be fine.

EXERCISE 10

A STILL POINT MEDITATION

• Find somewhere to sit where you feel comfortable, either indoors or outside.

• Close your eyes and tune into your body and how it is feeling. Adjust your posture if you feel any discomfort.

• Bring your attention to the breath, just observing its natural rhythm without attempting to deliberately slow it down (this will happen by itself).

• Be aware of the rise and fall of the abdomen… rising with the inbreath… and falling with the outbreath…

• If your attention wanders (as it inevitably will at first), gently bring the mind back to the breath, without judgement.

• Stay with the breath until you feel calm and at ease.

• When you feel ready, picture yourself there, as if you were an observer. Send yourself loving kindness and compassion.

• Whatever has been happening to you in your life, this is the time to drop all self-judgement, and just be with yourself.

• This is the time to rest, and be still, without self-analysis or blame.

• Perhaps you could visualize being seated within a sort of egg, or cocoon, protecting and nourishing you, preparing you to be born into a new world, a new phase of your life.

• Right now it is enough just to be at peace, a haven of tranquillity and calm.

• Breathing in... breathing out... breathing in... breathing out...

• Become aware of the pause between each breath as well as the breaths themselves.

• Recognize that you now sit between the rhythms of your own life, and this is an opportunity to dwell in that void, to seize the chance to cherish yourself, to give yourself some love, and honour your own humanity.

• Gradually, in a time of your own choosing, bring your awareness back to where you are, connect back with your body, and slowly open your eyes.

• Resolve to try to reconnect with this feeling of calm and peace within yourself whenever future times become difficult, and you feel swept up with the struggles of life. Inside each one of us is a core of tranquillity and peace; this meditation will help to strengthen it.

AND SO THE WHEEL TURNS

◆

'Still we must trust the goings on and stirrings under the
earth. We need not dig up the seeds and shine a light on them
to see if they are indeed growing. They need their quiet, restful
time of darkness to send out their roots. There are times in
our life for acceptance and nurture, when digging holes in the
psyche is inappropriate and can even disturb growth. And there
are times in our gardens for contemplation, rest, and dormancy.'

FROM 'CULTIVATING SACRED SPACE: GARDENING
FOR THE SOUL' BY ELIZABETH MURRAY
POMEGRANATE, 1997

◆

*This is truly a significant time of year, the crack between the worlds
of the inner life and outer manifestation. Nature is holding her
breath, awaiting the signal – of the sun's imminent return.*

IN THE MEANTIME, THE LESSON FOR US is to practise patience,
and to use this quiet time to rest, reflect and recuperate
our energy, knowing full well that it won't be too long before
we'll be out and about.

Out in the garden, the first spears of next spring's bulbs
are showing as they pierce the gap between dark and light.
Shrubs like mahonia, viburnum and winter jasmine are in
flower, and sarcococca and the winter-flowering honeysuckle
are getting ready to regale our noses with their delicious

scent. Hellebores are almost ready to entice us with their drooping flowers, which so light up the winter garden. Lungworts too are beginning to bring patches of blue or pink to the overly brown canvas, and the odd primrose, here and there, maybe adding a touch of yellow to the palette.

All of these floral contributions are, of course, very welcome, and it is understandable that we get excited at a new manifestation of the almost imperceptible gathering of the light, but we mustn't forget that this is still the heart of the winter. The ground is supposed to be bare, growth is supposed to be minimal, and sparseness is meant to be the norm. We need to calmly bide our time.

Dawning of a New Year

What there is at this time of year is an ever-increasing feeling of unseen stirrings underfoot. It is almost as if some giant underground creature is just awakening from deep slumber, ready to arise through the earth and greet the day refreshed, rubbing his eyes from forgotten dreams in the dark of the night. There is a palpable feeling of expectation and hesitant change in the air, and in our hearts and minds. This sense of change is boosted by the fact that this is also the time when we say goodbye to one year and welcome in the next, with all the optimism that usually entails.

The month of January derives its name from the Roman god Janus (pronounced 'yanus'), the guardian of gateways, who oversaw beginnings and endings. Although the name is Latin, the root (as is the case for most Indo-European languages) comes from Sanskrit, from the word 'yana' meaning 'transitional movement'. This is exactly the right time to review the old year, and preview the next. New Year's Eve is perfect for going through this process. It is also, of course, the time when we make our New Year's resolutions, a tradition to which, personally, I have always given a lot of thought and preparation. This is where we can exercise our resolve, looking at ways we can improve ourselves and the quality of our lives. However, with some of our most intractable character traits it can certainly test our resolution!

> 'We have only now, only this single eternal moment opening and unfolding before us day and night. To see this truth is to realize that the sacred and secular cannot be divided. Even the most transcendent visions of spirituality must shine through the here and now and be brought to life in how we walk, eat, and love one another.'
>
> FROM 'A PATH WITH HEART' BY JACK KORNFIELD
> BANTAM BOOKS, 1993

Watching the Waves of Desire

In the garden, this is a prime time to take a look at what worked and what didn't in the past twelve months, and to plan ways to optimize our plots in the next. This process is greatly aided by the avid perusal of the shiny new catalogues from various nurseries and seed companies, which promptly drop through the letterbox as if by magic, with the sole intention to lead us into temptation – and they inevitably do. All those colourful pictures of summer floral abundance can often prove just too irresistible.

What a great opportunity to be aware of our desiring nature! We can observe closely our reactions to the pictures in the catalogue, and watch how craving arises. It's an interesting process, seeing how our mind waters seeds of necessity within us, and suddenly our lives would not be complete without this particular rose bush, or that exact rhododendron, and before we know it we're filling in the order form.

However, being wise to this, if we don't feed this compulsion, and just sit with it for a while, we will soon bear witness to it simply fading away as the mind finds something else with which to be tempted. Now I am not suggesting that you just ignore any of the products on offer – after all, we all seek to replenish our beloved gardens with new plants on a fairly regular basis, and long may that continue. This is simply just an exercise for the mindful gardener to consider, whenever prevailed upon by any number of commercial companies, horticultural or otherwise. Not only may it serve as a further opportunity for mindfulness, but it also may save us a few pennies in the process!

If we try to view the world from a molecular level, any idea of things being separate simply cannot be sustained. When we look out at other people they seem to be separate, but the spaces between us consist of air molecules (as well as all the other unseen phenomena such as electromagnetic rays and radio waves). These molecules are in constant motion and interact with anything with which they come into contact, including our clothes and skin. Our breaths mingle, and the sounds we make ripple outwards, affecting all within hearing range. Our emotions affect our bodies and the people around us, and often fuel an emotional reaction from them, which in turn affects us. Everywhere, all over the cosmos, there is this eternal exchange of energy, which is so universally ubiquitous that it is absolutely impossible to say that one particular effect

'Every subatomic interaction consists of the annihilation of the original particles and the creation of new subatomic particles. The subatomic world is a continual dance of creation and annihilation, of mass changing into energy and energy changing into mass. Transient forms sparkle in and out of existence, creating a never-ending, forever newly created reality.'

FROM 'THE DANCING WU LI MASTERS' BY GARY ZUKAV
BANTAM BOOKS, 1980

has only one particular cause. It would probably be more true to say that everything is because everything else is. A butterfly flapping its wings in Peru really does have an effect on a tropical storm in the Indian Ocean.

So when it comes to performing tasks in the garden, try to be aware of this. There really is no separation between you, as the doer, and the action being done. The garden and the gardener are truly one. Rather than thinking of yourself as an outsider entering the space of the garden seeking to impose your will upon the helpless inhabitants, try to see it more as a dance of equals, wherein both may benefit. Adopt an attitude of service to the greater good, and you will reap the rewards.

THE SPIRIT OF RESOLUTION

◆

Some of my most favoured winter memories have been of walking briskly in the crisp air, with the sun shining in a clear blue sky, with the promise of a whole new year ahead of me. My resolve is fresh, and I feel solid in my determination to follow it through!

MAYBE IT'S SOMETHING ABOUT THE SHEER EXHILARA- TION of feeling so alive during these times that they are some of my most treasured experiences of being very much present in the here and now, so much so that I actually prefer this time of year to the heat of summer.

I have already mentioned the opportunity that the New Year can present to us regarding the chance to start afresh. The wheel of the year has truly turned and, with the promise of gradually lighter days to come, the spirit of resolution is in the air. Now is the time to plan ahead to achieve an even more colourful and/or productive garden. In line with this, there are a number of jobs still to do in order to reach this goal.

A Late Mulch

If there are beds that haven't been mulched yet, and are hence bare, then providing it's not been too frosty it is certainly a good idea to replenish the soil with the addition of composted organic material in order to put back lost fertility and build up soil structure. If, however, it is a frosty spell, then the work can still be done, remembering to leave the ground only rough dug, or rather forked, as the frost will work on the large clods of earth and hopefully break them down into a more workable tilth. This is because by doing so we are exposing much more surface area for the frosts to work upon, and the water in the soil, as it freezes, will shatter it into smaller particles. If the winter has been fairly mild throughout, then the addition of a mulch laid on the surface would not go amiss at any time. If beds are not intended for cultivation for some time it is a good idea to cover it with a sheet mulch, such as an old carpet or weighed-down cardboard. This will not only warm up the soil, but also suppress weeds at the same time.

> 'We had a small garden beside our house: it
> was a fairyland to me, where miracles of beauty
> were of everyday occurrence. Every morning at
> an early hour I would run out of my bed to greet
> the first pink flush of dawn through the trembling
> leaves of the coconut trees which stood in a line
> along the garden boundary. The dewdrops glistened
> as the grass caught the first tremor of the morning
> breeze. The sky seemed to bring a personable
> companionship, and my whole body drank in the
> light and peace of those silent hours. I was anxious
> never to miss a single morning, because each one
> was more precious to me than gold to a miser.'
>
> QUOTE BY RABINDRANATH TAGORE FROM 'CATHEDRALS OF
> THE SPIRIT: THE MESSAGE OF SACRED PLACES' BY T.C. MCLUHAN
> THORSONS, 1996

Preparing the Ground

To prepare the ground for early planting, especially on the
allotment or in the kitchen garden, it is a good idea to place
cloches on the surface in order to warm up the soil. This can
be in the form of either glass or plastic bells or other struc-
tures; anything, in fact, that will help to create the necessary
microclimate. It is amazing what a difference in temperature
simple devices like these can achieve.

If you have a greenhouse then this is an excellent time to give it a good clean, paying particular attention to the glass panes, as the clearer they are the stronger your seedlings will grow due to more efficient photosynthesis. Again, this is a good time to consider the fact that by acting now you are directly linked to the future health and well-being of the plants in your care. Even though these plants haven't as yet come into manifestation, their formation is dependent upon various conditions being met, including those that you, as the gardener, provide for them, and by taking the time to clean the greenhouse, or equivalent, you can assure that they come into the world with the optimum conditions possible.

Shedding Negative Energy

Following on from the greenhouse, it is a natural progression to switch your attention to the shed, if you have one. Starting afresh would entail bringing everything out into the light of day and sorting through what's needed, and what's not. It is very easy to accumulate all manner of things in a shed during the course of the year, and clearing out is best done now, before the coming spring brings the inevitable flurry of activity. Procrastination is not an option, as unused stuff is negative energy, and just like our inner process of letting go of whatever no longer serves us, so too is it mirrored in all those places, like sheds, wherein we tend to deposit stuff we'd rather not deal with, and hope nobody notices!

Any bird boxes, or other wildlife nests, can be cleaned out now before the parents go house-hunting. They are less likely to take up residence if the boxes are full of the remnants of last season's faecal matter, moulds and dead woodlice. There is generally no need to use chemical disinfectants as the smell may well put them off. I tend just to use an old toothbrush.

Room to Expand

One other job well worth doing is checking tree ties. I have learnt from past experience that if this is overlooked then trees can be strangled as they expand during their active growing phase. This is also true with shrubs whose labels are tied on with wire. What happens is that the cambium layer, which lies directly underneath the bark and through which nutrients flow, gets ring-barked all the way around the trunk and vital energy then drains away above the cut, and all of the top growth soon dies.

Sometimes, if the cut is not all around the trunk or branch, the tree or shrub may struggle on, as a minimum amount of nutrient is still able to squeeze through, but there is often not enough to sustain all of the top growth, and visible signs of stress will soon become apparent. If the worst does happen then the only course of action is for all of the growth above the tie to be cut away, and hopefully, with a little time, the relieved plant should recover, although you may not immediately get the original shape for which you had hoped.

THE GLIMMERING OF THE GREEN

◆

The land is still wrapped in the arms of winter chill, and the days are often grey and gloomy, but below the ground hardy perennials are stirring from their dark slumbers as their roots tentatively venture into action, searching for nutrients to break the fast of plants still dreamily dozing as dormancy begins slowly to dissipate.

LUNGWORTS AND WINTER CYCLAMEN are now coming well into flower, and early crocuses are beginning to put on a display, as are the delightful dwarf irises, with their rich colours and seemingly delicate forms. Here and there amid the brown mantle of winter there are hints of green appearing, heralding the nascent spring.

'When the ice of winter holds the house in its rigid grip, when curtains are drawn early against that vast frozen waste of landscape, almost like a hibernating hedgehog I relish the security of being withdrawn from all that summer ferment that is long since past. Then is the time for reappraisal: to spread out, limp and receptive, and let garden thoughts rise to the surface. They emerge from some deep source of stillness which the very fact of winter has released.'

FROM 'A GENTLE PLEA FOR CHAOS' BY MIRABEL OSLER
BLOOMSBURY, 1989

The heavenly scents of mahonia, viburnum, sarcococca, witch hazel and the gorgeous daphne waft through the cold air. Sensory delights like these seem almost out of place in the bareness of the winter garden, but they are nonetheless very welcome. By now the snowdrops are ringing out the message that change is truly in the air.

A Test of Patience

At this time of the year I must admit I do sometimes feel a little too impatient for the process of awakening to speed up. I guess this is common for lots of gardeners, eager as we are to get on with our horticultural endeavours. I consider myself

> 'True happiness comes from mindfulness.
> Mindfulness helps us to recognize the many conditions
> of happiness that are available in the here and in the
> now. Concentration helps us to get in touch more
> deeply with these conditions. With enough mindfulness
> and concentration, insight is born. With deep insight,
> we don't get angry any more, we don't despair any
> more, and we can enjoy each moment of life.'
>
> FROM 'BUDDHA MIND, BUDDHA BODY: WALKING TOWARD
> ENLIGHTENMENT' BY THICH NHAT HANH
> PARALLAX PRESS, 2007

a fairly patient individual, usually quite happy to wait for the circle of the year to spin at its own speed, but January nearly always seems to drag on beyond its allotted thirty-one days. So I suppose I should be grateful for the lessons it teaches me about true inner patience and forbearance. There isn't really a great deal to do in the garden, other than preparatory work, so my advice would be to take full advantage of this space in the diary, and just chill out. Enjoy the opportunity while you can, for spring is just around the corner, and you'll soon have your hands full again!

Full Circle

So, now we have come virtually full circle, from the snow-drops of the previous year to the snowdrops of the next. I cannot think of a more fitting flower with which to symbolize the wheel of the year, and this is why I have chosen it to act as a marker in the horticultural calendar.

I hope, within this book, that I have given you some useful pointers in how to bring a little more mindfulness to this great art of gardening. Horticulture is an activity that brings great opportunity for meditative practice, and I hope that, in however small a way, you will find this to be so.

Horticulture is an activity
that brings great opportunity for
meditative practice.

INDEX

DEDICATION & ACKNOWLEDGEMENTS

◆

To Collette Barnard, just for being.

I wish to acknowledge my best friend and life partner, Collette, for her love and support, and my colleagues at Chalice Well Gardens for their encouragement. For my spiritual support, the UK Community of Interbeing, and my Dharma brothers and sisters in my local Touching The Earth Sangha. And finally, my beloved spiritual teacher, the Venerable Thich Nhat Hanh, to whom I bow in gratitude.

BIBLIOGRAPHY

◆

Dharma Gaia: A Harvest of Essays in Buddhism and Ecology, edited by Allan Hunt Badiner (Parallax Press, 1990)

Each Moment is the Universe: Zen and the Way of Being Time by Dainin Katagiri (Shambhala Publications, 2007)

Sacred Celebrations: A Sourcebook by Glennie Kindred (Gothic Image, 2004)

The Alchemist's Journey: A New System for a New Age by Glennie Kindred (Hay House, 2005)

A Path with Heart by Jack Kornfield (Bantam Books 1993)

Thinking Like a Mountain: Towards a Council of All Beings by John Seed, Joanna Macy, Pat Fleming & Arne Naess (Heretic Books, 1988)

The Rebirth of Nature: The Greening of Science and God by Rupert Sheldrake (Park Street Press, 1994)

Essential Zen by Kazuaki Tanahashi & David Schneider (Castle Books, 1994)

Cultivating the Mind by Thich Nhat Hanh (Parallax Press, 1996)

Buddha Mind, Buddha Body by Thich Nhat Hanh (Parallax Press, 2007)

You Are Here by Thich Nhat Hanh (Shambhala Press, 2009)

Together We Are One by Thich Nhat Hanh (Parallax Press, 2010)